celebrating
PANCAKES
WAFFLES & CRÊPES

By

Avner Laskin

A LEISURE ARTS PUBLICATION

President and Chief Executive Officer: Rick Barton
Vice President and Chief Operations Officer: Tom Siebenmorgen
Vice President of Sales: Mike Behar
Director of Finance and Administration: Laticia Mull Dittrich
National Sales Director: Martha Adams
Creative Services: Chaska Lucas
Information Technology Director: Hermine Linz
Controller: Francis Caple
Vice President, Operations: Jim Dittrich
Retail Customer Service Manager: Stan Raynor
Print Production Manager: Fred F. Pruss
Editor-in-Chief: Susan White Sullivan
Director of Designer Relations: Cheryl Johnson
Special Projects Director: Susan Frantz Wiles
Art Publications Director: Rhonda Shelby
Senior Prepress Director: Mark Hawkins

Produced for Leisure Arts, Inc. by Penn Publishing Ltd.
www.penn.co.il
Editor-in-Chief: Rachel Penn
Editor: Shoshana Brickman
Culinary editing: Tamar Zakut
Design and layout: Ariane Rybski
Photography by: Daniel Lailah
Food styling: Amit Farber

PRINTED IN CHINA

ISBN-13: 978-1-60900-277-0
Library of Congress Control Number: 2011926744

Cover photography by Daniel Lailah

Contents

Introduction

About the Book

Pancakes, waffles and crêpes are such wonderful foods. Easy to make, versatile and satisfying, they can be served at any time of day and with virtually any topping. All you need is a few pantry staples and some basic kitchen appliances, and you're ready to go.

Celebrating Pancakes, Waffles & Crêpes gives you all the basic information you need to get started, plus lots of inspiration to keep you going. If you're a beginner, you'll find several basic recipes to choose from. Find the ones you like, and use them as your base.

When it comes to the toppings and fillings, don't be afraid to mix and match. A topping that's in the pancake section may be perfect for a batch of warm waffles. Use your imagination (and your appetite) as a guide, and enjoy!

About the Author

Avner Laskin is an experienced chef and author who has written cookbooks on everything from ice cream and chocolate to tomatoes and chickpeas. He studied at the prestigious Cordon Bleu Academy in Paris, where he received the Grand Diplôme de Cuisine and Pâtisserie. Laskin later specialized in traditional breads under the world-renowned Jean-Louis Clément at the Lenôtre School in Paris, and was awarded the coveted Diplôme de Pain de Tradition et de Qualité in 1998.

Laskin's culinary career includes internships at two-star Michelin restaurants in France and Germany, as well as extensive work as a restaurant consultant, specializing in kitchen design and recipe and menu development.

In **Celebrating Pancakes, Waffles and Crêpes**, Laskin expresses his love for these favorite dishes by presenting eclectic innovations alongside traditional treats.

Pancakes

A Few Golden Rules

Basic Pancakes

Classic Pancakes
Yeast Pancakes
Light & Fluffy Pancakes
Multigrain Pancakes
Whole-Wheat Pancakes
Egg-Free Pancakes
Gluten-Free Pancakes
Sweet Ricotta Pancakes

Sweet Pancake Dishes

Banana & Apple Pancakes
Pancake Cake
Layered Berry Pancakes
Pancakes with Dried Fruit
Pancakes with Fresh Mango Yogurt
Chocolate Sundae Pancakes
Pancakes with Grape Salad & Ricotta
Fresh & Festive Pineapple Coconut Pancakes
Pancakes with Fresh Apricot Jam
Jam & Granola Pancakes
Pancakes with Blueberries & Vanilla Ice Cream
Pancakes with Fresh Marmalade & Sugared Apples
Butter & Berry Jam Pancakes
Golden Banana Pancakes
Orange Jam & Crème Fraîche Pancakes
Pancakes with Strawberries & Crème Fraîche
Caramelized Coffee Pancakes
Ricotta Pancakes with Tropical Fruit Salad

Savory Pancake Dishes

Pancakes with Anchovy Spread
Ham 'n' Cheese Pancakes
Corn Pancakes
Pancakes with Bacon & Eggs
Cream Cheese & Salmon Pancakes
Pancakes with Roquefort Cheese & Roasted Walnuts
Pancakes with Spiced Corn & Grated Cheese
Cream Cheese & Caviar Pancakes
Goat Cheese & Tapenade Pancakes

Pancakes: A Few Golden Rules

Pancakes. They're satisfying, comforting and indulgent. They can be plain and simple or dressed up for guests. They can be anything you want them to be, and more than you imagined! Beloved by children and adults alike, they are a great food for kids to make on their own.

In our kitchen, the smell of pancakes is the smell of weekend mornings. I usually make pancakes with a whisk, and there is something about that energetic whisking that is magical. Even the sound of the whisk is just right to me—music to my ears on a quiet weekend.

Try out the basic recipes until you find the one that you and your family like best. Once you find that recipe, use it often, simply changing the toppings to create a different meal. You can use your favorite family recipe for all of the dishes in this chapter, or experiment with the pancake recipes that I suggest.

COOKING

• How you cook your pancakes depends on the pan or griddle you're using and the size of pancakes you want to make. In most cases, you'll heat the pan over medium heat and then grease it with butter or oil. After the first greasing, you usually won't need to grease the pan again as you cook.

• After the pan is warm, pour in several pools of batter, 2 inches apart. You'll need about 2 tablespoons of batter to make a 2½-inch pancake. If you are using a plett pan, fill each cavity about two-thirds full.

• After about 30 seconds, the batter will begin to set. You'll see the edges of the pancake begin to dry and bubbles will start forming on the top. When you see small bubbles in the middle of the pancake, it's time to flip it.

• Slide a spatula under the pancake and check the bottom. If it is a nice golden color, flip the pancake and cook it on the other side for about 30 seconds.

• Keep your eyes on the pancakes as they cook. If they aren't firming up and there are no bubbles on top, the heat is too low. If the pan is smoking, the heat is too high.

• The first pancake usually doesn't come out quite right. If it's too dark or too light, adjust the heat accordingly. Taste the pancake and check the flavor. I don't recommend adjusting the batter at this stage, but you can definitely adjust the topping by adding a bit more (or a bit less) sugar.

EQUIPMENT

A few essentials are important for making your pancakes delicious:

Sifter Use this to sift the flour and baking powder to ensure that the batter is airy and lump-free. If you don't have a sifter, use a fine-mesh colander.

Whisk This is crucial for combining ingredients, but you can also use an electric mixer. If you do, run it on low speed after the dry and wet ingredients have been combined.

Pancake griddle or nonstick (ceramic or silicon-coated) frying pan with low sides and a thick bottom You can use either of these to cook your pancakes. I recommend using a relatively large pan (mine has a 12½-inch diameter) so you can make several pancakes at one time. The low sides make it easier to work with a spatula.

Small ladle Use this to transfer the batter to the frying pan.

Plett pan This is a Swedish pan with round cavities that produces evenly-shaped round pancakes. You can also use metallic rings (like those used to make poached eggs) to make pancakes that are perfect spheres.

Long, thin silicon spatula This is crucial for flipping pancakes with ease.

INGREDIENTS

• Read every recipe in advance, from start to finish, and make sure you have all the ingredients.

• For best results, use fresh butter, eggs and milk, and choose pure vanilla extract.

• In all of the recipes, you may use either oil or butter, both in the batter and for greasing. The conversion is 1:1. If you choose butter, make sure it's fresh. If you use oil, select a vegetable oil that doesn't have a dominant taste.

• White sugar may be replaced with an equal quantity of brown sugar.

• All-purpose white flour may be partially replaced with whole-wheat flour. Since whole-wheat flour tends to be a bit heavier than white flour, I recommend replacing only half of the white flour. If you do this, increase the liquids by about 15 to 20 percent.

• Milk can be replaced with coconut milk, soy milk, rice milk or even fruit juice. For an even greater indulgence, the milk can be partly replaced with sweet cream. The result is delightful, but browns more quickly.

• Once you add the dry ingredients, make sure that you don't overmix the batter. This ensures a light and fluffy texture.

• Pancake batter should be smooth and thick, similar to heavy cream. If the batter is too thin, add a bit more flour. If the batter is too thick, this is a bit more problematic, since adding more water or milk to batter that has already been mixed can damage the texture.

• In most of the basic recipes, the batter must rest at room temperature for at least 30 minutes. Though it may be tempting to skip this stage (especially if you have hungry children waiting for breakfast), this stage is important since it allows for the fermentation process to begin. This helps create that authentic pancake flavor.

• Every recipe in this book produces about thirty-two 2½-inch pancakes. Of course, you can make the pancakes larger or smaller, or double the recipe size with ease.

REHEATING & FREEZING

• Ideally, pancakes should be served soon after cooking. To keep pancakes warm and moist before serving, stack them on a plate and cover the stack with a towel.

• Pancakes can be frozen for up to 1 week. If you plan on freezing pancakes, first cool them to room temperature, then place them in an airtight container. Frozen pancakes can be defrosted on the countertop or in the microwave.

SERVING

• Pancakes should be served warm. You can reheat them in a microwave or wrap them in aluminum foil and place them in a warm oven for about 3 minutes.

• There are countless ways to dress up pancakes. You can serve them with toppings on the side or integrate tasty additions into the pancakes as they cook.

• If you choose the second option, don't mix the additions into the batter. Instead, start cooking the pancake in the pan; when the bottom sets and the top starts to bubble, sprinkle in the additions. Follow your taste buds and use your imagination! Here are some ideas to help you get started:

- thawed frozen berries—place them in a colander first to drain off any liquid
- dried fruit—soak the fruit in boiling water for 10 minutes first, then chop into chunks and place in a colander to drain off any liquid
- chopped nuts
- chopped fresh herbs
- grated lemon or orange rind
- cocoa

For a fabulous pancake brunch, put a variety of toppings on the table and invite your guests to customize their serving. Serve fresh fruit, grilled fruit, caramelized or liquor-soaked fruit, fresh or roasted nuts, crème fraîche, whipped cream, peanut butter and whatever else takes your fancy.

YEAST PANCAKES

Keep the following tips in mind when making the pancakes on page 13:

• Use lukewarm water to invigorate and accelerate the activity of the yeast.

• Mix the liquids first and then add the dry ingredients.

• To ensure that the batter is lump-free, use one of the following appliances to whisk the ingredients: a hand whisk, an electric mixer fitted with a whisk attachment, or a food processor fitted with a plastic whisk.

• Let the mixture rest for at least 1 hour after mixing to allow the yeast to start fermenting.

• When spooning the batter onto the frying pan, make sure you don't pop the air bubbles that formed while the batter was resting. These bubbles help make the pancakes so light and fluffy.

Classic Pancakes

Serves

4

This recipe produces a fantastic pancake with ease. It requires the most basic of ingredients—items most people already have stocked in their kitchens.

INGREDIENTS

1½ cups all-purpose white flour

1 teaspoon baking powder

3 tablespoons powdered sugar

Pinch of salt

2 large eggs

3 tablespoons canola oil, plus more for greasing

1½ cups cold milk

½ teaspoon pure vanilla extract

PREPARATION

1. In a large bowl, sift together the flour, baking powder, powdered sugar and salt.

2. Whisk the eggs and oil into the mixture. Add the milk and vanilla gradually, while stirring, until batter is thick and smooth.

3. Cover the mixture with plastic wrap and let it rest for 30 minutes before cooking.

4. Heat a large nonstick frying pan over medium heat and brush with a thin coating of oil. Pour 2 or 3 tablespoons of batter onto the pan in three different places, leaving space between each pancake so that they do not stick together.

5. Cook until the bottom of the pancake is golden and there are bubbles on the surface of the pancake, a few of which have burst. Using a long thin spatula, flip each pancake and cook for another 1 or 2 minutes. When the pancakes are golden on both sides, arrange in a stack on a large plate and cover with a clean cloth.

6. Repeat with the remaining batter. Serve immediately or store, covered with aluminum foil or parchment paper, for up to 20 minutes in a warm oven.

Yeast Pancakes

Serves

4

When making yeast pancakes, I prefer using a flat frying pan rather than a plett pan so the pancakes can rise to their hearts' content! This batter can be prepared a full day in advance. If you decide to do this, there is no need to let the batter rise (in step 4).

INGREDIENTS

2 tablespoons fresh yeast or 2 teaspoons dry yeast

⅔ cup lukewarm water

⅔ cup cold milk

2 large eggs

1½ cups all-purpose white flour

2 tablespoons powdered sugar

Pinch of salt

2 tablespoons melted butter, plus more for greasing

½ teaspoon pure vanilla extract

PREPARATION

1. In a large bowl, dissolve the yeast in the water. Mix in the milk and eggs.

2. Sift the flour and powdered sugar into a small bowl, and then mix in the salt.

3. Add the flour mixture to the yeast mixture, whisking until the batter becomes thick and smooth. Whisk in butter and vanilla.

4. Cover the mixture with plastic wrap and let it rest in a warm area for at least 1 hour.

5. When the mixture has risen and is full of air bubbles, it's ready to be cooked.

6. Heat a large nonstick frying pan over medium heat and brush with a thin coating of butter. Pour 2 or 3 tablespoons of batter onto the pan in three different places, leaving space between each pancake so that they do not stick together.

7. Cook until the bottom of the pancake is golden and there are bubbles on the surface of the pancake, a few of which have burst. Using a long thin spatula, flip each pancake and cook for another 1 or 2 minutes. When the pancakes are golden on both sides, arrange in a stack on a large plate and cover with a clean cloth.

8. Repeat with the remaining batter. Serve immediately or store, covered with aluminum foil or parchment paper, for up to 20 minutes in a warm oven.

Light & Fluffy Pancakes

Serves

4

It's the whipped egg whites that contribute to the fluffiness in this pancake recipe. There's no need to let the batter rest before cooking, since you want to enjoy the fluffiness of the egg whites.

INGREDIENTS

1 cup cold milk

½ teaspoon pure vanilla extract

3 tablespoons powdered sugar

Pinch of salt

4 large eggs, separated

1½ cups all-purpose white flour

1 teaspoon baking powder

2 tablespoons canola oil, plus more for greasing

PREPARATION

1. In a large bowl, combine the milk, vanilla, powdered sugar and salt. Using a hand or stand mixer, add the egg yolks and mix well.

2. Sift together the flour and baking powder, and then gradually add to the batter, mixing constantly. Continue mixing until the batter is thick and smooth.

3. Stir in the oil until completely blended, then set aside.

4. In the bowl of an electric mixer, whip the egg whites at high speed until soft and foamy.

5. Using a rubber spatula, gently fold the whipped egg whites into the batter.

6. Heat a large nonstick frying pan over medium heat and brush with a thin coating of oil. Pour 2 or 3 tablespoons of batter onto the pan in three different places, leaving space between each pancake so that they do not stick together.

7. Cook until the bottom of the pancake is golden and there are bubbles on the surface of the pancake, a few of which have burst. Using a long thin spatula, flip each pancake and cook for another 1 or 2 minutes. When the pancakes are golden on both sides, arrange in a stack on a large plate and cover with a clean cloth.

8. Repeat with the remaining batter. Serve immediately or store, covered with aluminum foil or parchment paper, for up to 20 minutes in a warm oven.

Multigrain Pancakes

Serves

4

This is a terrific option for people who love the flavor of nutty grains. It results in a more satisfying pancake that's fantastic, either sweet or savory.

INGREDIENTS

¼ cup sesame seeds

2 tablespoons flax seeds

2 tablespoons rolled oats

1½ cups all-purpose white flour

1 teaspoon baking powder

3 tablespoons powdered sugar

Pinch of salt

4 large eggs

2 tablespoons canola oil, plus more for greasing

2 cups cold milk

½ teaspoon pure vanilla extract

PREPARATION

1. In an electric grinder, or using a pestle, grind the sesame seeds, flax seeds and rolled oats until they are finely ground.

2. In a large bowl, sift together flour, baking powder, powdered sugar and salt. Mix in the ground oat mixture until combined.

3. Whisk the eggs and oil into the flour mixture, and then gradually add the milk and vanilla. Continue stirring until the batter is thick and smooth.

4. Cover the mixture with plastic wrap and let it rest for 30 minutes.

5. Heat a large nonstick frying pan over medium heat and brush with a thin coating of oil. Pour 2 or 3 tablespoons of batter onto the pan in three different places, leaving space between each pancake so that they do not stick together.

6. Cook until the bottom of the pancake is golden and there are bubbles on the surface of the pancake, a few of which have burst. Using a long thin spatula, flip each pancake and cook for another 1 or 2 minutes. When the pancakes are golden on both sides, arrange in a stack on a large plate and cover with a clean cloth.

7. Repeat with the remaining batter. Serve immediately or store, covered with aluminum foil or parchment paper, for up to 20 minutes in a warm oven.

Whole-Wheat Pancakes

Serves

4

Here's an excellent pancake recipe for people watching their intake of white flour. It's also a great healthier treat for kids, since they probably won't notice the difference.

INGREDIENTS

1¼ cups whole-wheat flour

1 teaspoon baking powder

3 tablespoons powdered sugar

Pinch of salt

4 large eggs

3 tablespoons melted butter, plus more for greasing

2 cups cold milk

½ teaspoon pure vanilla extract

PREPARATION

1. In a large bowl, sift together the flour, baking powder, powdered sugar and salt.

2. Whisk the eggs and melted butter into the flour mixture, and then gradually add the milk and vanilla, stirring constantly until the batter is thick and smooth.

3. Cover the mixture with plastic wrap and let it rest for 30 minutes.

4. Heat a large nonstick frying pan over medium heat and brush with a thin coating of butter. Pour 2 or 3 tablespoons of batter onto the pan in three different places, leaving space between each pancake so that they do not stick together.

5. Cook until the bottom of the pancake is golden and there are bubbles on the surface of the pancake, a few of which have burst. Using a long thin spatula, flip each pancake and cook for another 1 or 2 minutes.

6. When the pancakes are golden on both sides, arrange in a stack on a large plate and cover with a clean cloth.

7. Repeat with the remaining batter. Serve immediately or store, covered with aluminum foil or parchment paper, for up to 20 minutes in a warm oven.

Egg-Free Pancakes

4

This egg-free batter is a little on the sticky side, so use more butter than usual to grease the pan, and use a pan that's resistant to high heat.

INGREDIENTS

1 cup white all-purpose flour

1 teaspoon baking powder

1 tablespoon powdered sugar

Pinch of salt

1 cup cold milk

2 tablespoons melted butter, plus more for greasing

½ teaspoon pure vanilla extract

PREPARATION

1. In a large bowl, sift together the flour, baking powder, powdered sugar and salt.

2. Gradually whisk in the milk, butter, and vanilla and stir until the batter is thick and smooth.

3. Cover the mixture with plastic wrap and let it rest in the refrigerator for 30 minutes.

4. Heat a large nonstick frying pan over medium heat and brush with a thin coating of butter. Pour 2 or 3 tablespoons of batter onto the pan in three different places, leaving space between each pancake so that they do not stick together.

5. Cook until the bottom of the pancake is golden and there are bubbles on the surface of the pancake, a few of which have burst. Using a long thin spatula, flip each pancake and cook for another 1 or 2 minutes.

6. When the pancakes are golden on both sides, arrange in a stack on a large plate and cover with a clean cloth.

7. Repeat with the remaining batter. Serve immediately or store, covered with aluminum foil or parchment paper, for up to 20 minutes in a warm oven.

Gluten-Free Pancakes

Serves

4

Many people today eat gluten-free foods on a regular basis. With this recipe, homemade pancakes can be added to the list of permissible treats. Use tapioca flour, rice flour, or any other gluten-free flour.

INGREDIENTS

1 cup gluten-free flour

1 tablespoon gluten-free baking powder

2 tablespoons powdered sugar

½ teaspoon salt

2 large eggs

¼ cup melted butter, plus more for greasing

1 cup cold milk

1 teaspoon pure vanilla extract

PREPARATION

1. In a large bowl, sift together the flour, baking powder, and powdered sugar. Add the salt and mix well.

2. Whisk the eggs and melted butter into the flour mixture, and then gradually add the milk and vanilla, stirring constantly until the batter is thick and smooth.

3. Cover the mixture with plastic wrap and let it rest for 30 minutes.

4. Heat a large nonstick frying pan over medium heat and brush with a thin coating of butter. Pour 2 or 3 tablespoons of batter onto the pan in three different places, leaving space between each pancake so that they do not stick together.

5. Cook until the bottom of the pancake is golden and there are bubbles on the surface of the pancake, a few of which have burst. Using a long thin spatula, flip each pancake and cook for another 1 or 2 minutes.

6. When the pancakes are golden on both sides, arrange in a stack on a large plate and cover with a clean cloth.

7. Repeat with the remaining batter. Serve immediately or store, covered with aluminum foil or parchment paper, for up to 20 minutes in a warm oven.

Sweet Ricotta Pancakes

Serves

4

Ricotta is a lovely light white cheese that takes on flavors with elegance. Its flavor and texture both blend beautifully into the pancake batter.

INGREDIENTS

1½ cups all-purpose white flour

1 teaspoon baking powder

2 teaspoons powdered sugar

Pinch of salt

2 large eggs

3 teaspoons melted butter, plus more for greasing

1½ cups milk

½ teaspoon pure vanilla extract

7 ounces fresh ricotta cheese

Zest from 1 lemon

PREPARATION

1. In a large bowl, sift together the flour, baking powder, powdered sugar and salt.

2. Whisk the eggs and melted butter into the mixture, and then gradually add the milk and vanilla. Continue stirring until the batter is thick and smooth.

3. Cover the mixture with plastic wrap and let it rest in the refrigerator for 30 minutes.

4. After the batter has rested, mix in the ricotta cheese and lemon zest until evenly combined.

5. Heat a large nonstick frying pan over medium heat and brush with a thin coating of butter. Pour 2 or 3 tablespoons of batter onto the pan in three different places, leaving space between each pancake so that they do not stick together.

6. Cook until the bottom of the pancake is golden and there are bubbles on the surface of the pancake, a few of which have burst. Using a long thin spatula, flip each pancake and cook for another 1 or 2 minutes.

7. When the pancakes are golden on both sides, arrange in a stack on a large plate and cover with a clean cloth.

8. Repeat with the remaining batter. Serve immediately or store, covered with aluminum foil or parchment paper, for up to 20 minutes in a warm oven.

Banana & Apple Pancakes

Serves

6

These aromatic pancakes feature chunks of fresh apples and bananas. To create the lovely little round pancakes pictured here, use a plett pan (page 9).

INGREDIENTS

1 Golden Delicious apple, peeled, cored and cut into ½-inch dice

Juice from ½ lemon

1 cup all-purpose white flour

1 teaspoon baking powder

2 tablespoons powdered sugar

Pinch of salt

2 large eggs

2 tablespoons melted butter, plus more for greasing

1 cup cold milk

⅓ cup plain yogurt

½ teaspoon pure vanilla extract

1 banana

PREPARATION

1. Place the apple in a bowl and pour in the lemon juice. Add cold water to cover and set aside.

2. In a large bowl, sift together the flour, baking powder, sugar and salt.

3. Whisk the eggs and melted butter into the mixture, and then gradually add the milk, yogurt and vanilla while stirring, until batter is thick and smooth.

4. Cover the mixture with plastic wrap and let it rest in the refrigerator for 30 minutes.

5. Grease the pan cavities with butter and heat over medium heat.

6. Slice the banana in half lengthwise, and then slice each half into slices, ¼-inch wide.

7. Place 2 apple pieces and 2 banana pieces into each pan cavity, and cook for about 1 minute. Pour batter into each cavity to cover the fruit and cook for 1 or 2 minutes, or until pancakes are golden.

8. Flip the pancakes, using a thin flat spatula, and cook on the other side until golden. Transfer the pancakes to a serving dish.

9. Repeat with the remaining batter and serve.

Pancake Cake

6

Celebrate a birthday brunch with this beautiful pancake cake. If you prepare the apples in advance, mix them with a bit of lemon juice to prevent them from turning brown.

INGREDIENTS

3 Golden Delicious apples, peeled, cored and cut into chunks

Juice from ½ lemon

2 large eggs

¼ cup all-purpose white flour

½ teaspoon baking powder

Pinch of salt

1 tablespoon sugar

2 tablespoons oil, plus more for greasing

⅓ cup milk

2 tablespoons powdered sugar, for decoration

1 cup crème fraîche, for garnish

1 cup fresh strawberries, for garnish

PREPARATION

1. Place the apples in a bowl and pour in the lemon juice. Add cold water to cover and set aside.

2. In a medium bowl, whisk the eggs. Sift together the flour and baking powder, and then gradually add to the eggs, whisking as you add.

3. Whisk in the salt, sugar, oil and milk until smooth.

4. Cover the mixture with plastic wrap and let rest for at least 30 minutes in the refrigerator.

5. Transfer the apples to a colander to drain, and then mix into the batter.

6. Heat a large frying pan over low heat and brush with a thin coating of oil. Pour in the batter and cook for about 5 minutes. Using a long thin spatula, carefully flip over the pancake and cook on the other side for about 5 minutes.

7. When the pancake is golden on both sides, remove from the pan and place on a serving plate. Sift powdered sugar on top.

8. To serve, cut the pancake into wedges, and serve each wedge with a dollop of crème fraîche and strawberries.

Layered Berry Pancakes

Serves

 4

This decadent dessert is made with layers of delicate pancakes, sweet berry confit and tangy crème fraîche. The combination of colors and flavors is delightful.

INGREDIENTS

½ teaspoon lemon juice

3 tablespoons powdered sugar

¼ pound + ¼ pound frozen mixed berries

1 cup crème fraîche

1 batch Light and Fluffy Pancakes (page 14), stacked on a plate and covered with a cloth

½ pound fresh berries for decoration (optional)

PREPARATION

1. In a blender, combine the lemon juice, powdered sugar and ¼ pound of berries until mixture is a thick sauce. If you prefer smooth sauce, pour the mixture through a fine sieve strainer to remove the berry seeds.

2. Transfer the sauce to a bowl or glass jar. Mix in the remaining ¼ pound of berries and set the sauce aside.

3. To serve, place a pancake on a serving dish, top with a layer of crème fraîche, then a spoonful of berry sauce.

4. Repeat two more times, to create a triple layer.

5. Repeat to make four similar servings and serve.

Pancakes with Dried Fruit

4

This sauce is easy to make for anyone who keeps a stock of dried fruit in their pantry. Serve with plain yogurt for just the right combination of flavors.

INGREDIENTS

¼ cup finely chopped dried dates

¼ cup finely chopped dried apricots

¼ cup finely chopped light raisins

3 tablespoons fresh orange juice

1 tablespoon honey, plus more for drizzling

1 batch Whole-Wheat Pancakes (page 17), stacked on a plate and covered with a cloth

½ cup yogurt

PREPARATION

1. In a medium bowl, combine the dates, apricots, raisins, orange juice, and honey.

2. To serve, arrange the pancakes on individual serving dishes. Top each serving with equal amounts of the dried fruit mixture and yogurt, and drizzle honey over top. Serve immediately.

Pancakes with Fresh Mango Yogurt

Serves

4

Mango season isn't very long, so I like to make the most of it. In this recipe, I've added a bit of toasted coconut to create a really tropical treat.

INGREDIENTS

1 cup fresh mango chunks

½ teaspoon lemon juice

3 tablespoons powdered sugar

⅓ cup yogurt

1 batch Light and Fluffy Pancakes (page 14), stacked on a plate and covered with a cloth

2 tablespoons roasted coconut, for decoration

PREPARATION

1. In a food processor, blend the mango, lemon juice, sugar and yogurt until smooth.

2. To serve, arrange the pancakes on a serving dish and top evenly with the mango mixture. Sprinkle toasted coconut on top and serve.

Chocolate Sundae Pancakes

Serves 4

Looking for a really indulgent dessert? Look no further, since this dish features rich cream, sweet chocolate, creamy ice cream and delicious pancakes. All you need is someone to share it with!

INGREDIENTS

¾ cup heavy cream

2 tablespoons sugar

1 teaspoon vanilla extract

5 ounces semi-sweet chocolate

1 batch Classic Pancakes (page 12), stacked on a plate and covered with a cloth

8 scoops vanilla ice cream

PREPARATION

1. In a small saucepan over medium heat, bring the cream, sugar and vanilla just to the boiling point.

2. Remove from the heat and whisk in the chocolate until a smooth chocolate sauce forms.

3. To serve, arrange the pancakes on serving dishes and top with ice cream. Pour the chocolate sauce on top and serve immediately.

Pancakes with Grape Salad & Ricotta

Serves 4

Most types of cheese pair wonderfully with fresh grapes, and ricotta is no exception. Enhance the flavor of the grapes with a few basic spices and enjoy.

INGREDIENTS

½ pound seedless red grapes, halved

½ teaspoon lemon juice

2 tablespoons olive oil

½ teaspoon salt

1 teaspoon balsamic vinegar

1 batch Multigrain Pancakes (page 16), stacked on a plate and covered with a cloth

½ cup ricotta cheese

PREPARATION

1. In a medium bowl, gently combine the grapes, lemon juice, olive oil, salt and vinegar. Set aside.

2. To serve, arrange the pancakes on a serving dish and top with the grape mixture. Crumble some ricotta cheese on top, drizzle with olive oil, and serve.

Fresh & Festive Pineapple Coconut Pancakes

Serves

4

Fresh pineapple, a bit of liqueur and a batch of ricotta pancakes. That's all you need to create this impressive dessert.

INGREDIENTS

1 fresh pineapple, cut into ¼-inch wedges

2 tablespoons Piña Colada liqueur

1 batch Sweet Ricotta Pancakes (page 20), stacked on a plate and covered with a cloth

4 scoops coconut ice cream

1 tablespoon roasted coconut, for decoration

PREPARATION

1. Place the pineapple pieces in a shallow bowl and pour the liqueur on top. Set aside, leaving the pineapple to absorb the liqueur.

2. To serve, stack the pineapple wedges and pancakes on individual serving dishes. Top each stack with a scoop of ice cream, sprinkle with coconut, and serve immediately.

Pancakes with Fresh Apricot Jam

Serves

4

The topping in this recipe can be served with pancakes, waffles, crêpes, or fresh bread. It's a great winter jam, since it doesn't require fresh fruit.

INGREDIENTS

½ cup dark raisins

Boiling water

3 tablespoons sugar

½ pound dried apricots, cut into ¼-inch dice

½ teaspoon fresh lemon juice

1 batch Sweet Ricotta Pancakes (page 20), stacked on a plate and covered with a cloth

¼ cup yogurt

PREPARATION

1. Place the raisins in small cup and pour in boiling water to cover. Set aside to soak.

2. In a medium saucepan, cook the sugar over medium heat, until it becomes a light caramel.

3. Reduce the heat to low, add the apricots and lemon juice, and cook for 30 to 40 minutes, stirring regularly, until a thick jam forms. Remove from the heat and set aside.

4. To serve, arrange the pancakes on serving dishes and top with yogurt and fresh jam. Drain the raisins, sprinkle on top, and serve.

Fresh & Festive Pineapple Coconut Pancakes

Jam & Granola Pancakes

Jam & Granola Pancakes

4

This recipe makes a great, wholesome breakfast combo. Fresh fruity jam, crunchy granola and tangy yogurt along with whole-wheat pancakes—delicious!

INGREDIENTS

3 tablespoons white sugar

½ pound frozen mixed berries

1 batch Whole-Wheat Pancakes batter (page 17), stacked on a plate and covered with a cloth

½ cup granola

½ cup yogurt

PREPARATION

1. In a medium saucepan, cook sugar over medium heat until it turns a light caramel color.

2. Add the berries and cook over low heat for 30 to 40 minutes, until mixture becomes a thick jam. Remove from heat and set aside.

3. To serve, place a few pancakes in a stack and top with a teaspoon of fresh jam. Sprinkle with granola and serve with yogurt on the side.

Pancakes with Blueberries & Vanilla Ice Cream

Serves

4

This dish is a celebration of colors and flavor. Fresh blueberries, creamy ice cream, and a batch of silver dollar pancakes – what could be better? For a festive red-white-and-blue dessert, serve with some strawberries, too!

INGREDIENTS

1 batch Yeast Pancakes (page 13), stacked on a plate and covered with a cloth

8 scoops vanilla ice cream

½ pound fresh blueberries

1 tablespoon powdered sugar, for decoration

PREPARATION

1. Arrange the pancakes on a serving platter.

2. Top each pancake with a scoop of ice cream, and sprinkle with blueberries. Dust powdered sugar on top, and serve.

Pancakes with Fresh Marmalade & Sugared Apples

Serves

4

The sophisticated sweet tooth will delight in this dish, which features fresh orange marmalade, gently cooked apples and wholesome whole-wheat pancakes. The topping takes a while to prepare, so cook the pancakes while the topping is baking.

INGREDIENTS

4 very ripe oranges

3 tablespoons + ½ cup + ½ cup white sugar

½ cup water

2 Granny Smith apples, peeled, cored and cut into 1-inch dice

1 batch Whole-Wheat Pancakes batter (page 17), stacked on a plate and covered with a cloth

PREPARATION

1. Preheat the oven to 200°F and line a baking sheet with parchment paper.

2. Cut the oranges (with rind) into quarters. Remove the seeds, transfer to a food processor fitted with a metal blade, and pulse until a smooth paste forms.

3. In a medium saucepan, cook 3 tablespoons of the sugar over medium heat until it becomes a light caramel.

4. Reduce the heat to low, add the processed oranges, and cook for 30 to 40 minutes, until a thick jam forms. Remove from heat and set aside.

5. In a small saucepan, combine the water and ¼ cup of sugar and bring to a boil over medium heat. Add the apples, cook for 2 minutes, then remove from heat.

6. Sprinkle the remaining ¼ cup of sugar onto a large flat plate. Using a slotted spoon, remove the apples from the saucepan and place them on the sugar-coated plate.

7. Roll the apples in the sugar until they are coated, then transfer them to the baking sheet and bake for 50 minutes.

8. To serve, arrange a few pancakes on each serving dish and top with sugared apple chunks and marmalade.

Butter & Berry Jam Pancakes

Serves

4

Go back to the simpler pleasures in life, with basic foods such as fresh butter, fresh jam and fresh yeast pancakes. It's the quintessential comfort food.

INGREDIENTS

¼ cup softened butter, plus more for garnish

½ cup fresh mixed berries

1 tablespoon powdered sugar

1 batch Yeast Pancakes (page 13), stacked on a plate and covered with a cloth

PREPARATION

1. In a small bowl, combine the butter, berries and powdered sugar until well mixed. Set aside.

2. To serve, place a spoonful of the berry mixture on each pancake and serve with butter on the side.

Golden Banana Pancakes

Serves

4

Bananas are a great fruit for breakfast, since they give you energy for the entire day. Heating them gently before serving really brings out their sweetness.

INGREDIENTS

4 ripe bananas, cut into ¼-inch slices

¼ cup maple syrup

1 batch Light and Fluffy Pancakes (page 14), stacked on a plate and covered with a cloth

PREPARATION

1. Heat a nonstick frying pan over medium heat and gently sauté the banana slices until golden.

2. Add the maple syrup, remove from the heat, and set aside.

3. Arrange the pancakes on individual serving dishes and pour the banana syrup on top. Serve immediately.

Butter & Berry Jam Pancakes

Orange Jam
& Crème Fraîche Pancakes

Serves

4

Enjoy the simpler pleasures in life with this comforting dish. All you need is fresh butter, fresh berries, and some fresh yeast pancakes.

INGREDIENTS

5 oranges

3 tablespoons sugar

1 batch Yeast Pancakes (page 13), stacked on a plate and covered with a cloth

2 tablespoons powdered sugar, for garnish

PREPARATION

1. Cut 4 oranges (with rind) into quarters. Remove the seeds, transfer to a food processor fitted with a metal blade, and pulse until a smooth paste forms.

2. In a medium saucepan, heat the sugar over medium heat until it becomes a light caramel.

3. Reduce the heat to low, add the processed oranges and cook for 30 to 40 minutes, until a thick jam forms. Remove from heat and set aside to cool.

4. Cut the remaining orange into thick rounds.

5. To serve, arrange the pancakes onto individual serving dishes and sift powdered sugar on top.

6. Top with fresh marmalade and orange rounds, and serve immediately.

Pancakes with Strawberries & Crème Fraîche

Pancakes with Strawberries & Crème Fraîche

Serves

4

This dish is simple to make, but beautiful and tasty. To upgrade the presentation, just sprinkle on a bit of powdered sugar.

INGREDIENTS

½ pound wild strawberries, halved

1 tablespoon sugar

1 batch Yeast Pancakes (see page 13), stacked on a plate and covered with a cloth

½ cup crème fraîche

PREPARATION

1. Place the strawberries in a large bowl and top with the sugar.

2. Mix gently until the strawberries are evenly coated with sugar. Refrigerate until ready to use.

3. To serve, arrange the pancakes on individual serving dishes and top with strawberries and crème fraîche.

Caramelized Coffee Pancakes

Serves

4

This dish is definitely for an adult crowd. Coffee, coffee liqueur, and nutty ice cream. Sophisticated and sweet.

INGREDIENTS

¼ cup sugar

½ cup heavy cream

1 tablespoon quality instant coffee

1 tablespoon coffee liqueur

1 batch Classic Pancakes (page 12), stacked on a plate and covered with a cloth

8 scoops walnut ice cream

PREPARATION

1. In a small saucepan, heat the sugar over medium heat until golden.

2. Reduce the heat to low heat and mix in the cream and coffee. Cook, stirring constantly, until sauce is thick and smooth.

3. Remove from the heat, whisk in the liqueur, and set aside.

4. To serve, arrange the pancakes on individual serving dishes. Top with ice cream and pour the coffee sauce on top.

Ricotta Pancakes with Tropical Fruit Salad

Serves

4

It's always fun to serve special foods when guests arrive. In this dish, delicate ricotta pancakes are accompanied by a symphony of fresh tropical fruit.

INGREDIENTS

1 banana, cut into ¼-inch slices

1 fresh pineapple, peeled, cored, and cut into ¼-inch dice

1 guava, cut into ¼-inch dice

1 fresh star fruit, cut into ¼-inch dice

1 mango, peeled, pitted, and cut into ¼-inch dice

6 passion fruit, cut in half with pulp removed

1 tablespoon powdered sugar

1 batch Sweet Ricotta Pancakes (page 20), stacked on a plate and covered with a cloth

PREPARATION

1. In a large bowl, mix together the banana, pineapple, guava, star fruit, mango and passion fruit. Sprinkle in the sugar.

2. To serve, arrange the pancakes on individual serving dishes, and top with the fruit mixture.

Pancakes with Anchovy Spread

Serves

4

Anchovies, that surprisingly salty fish that lends a distinct flavor to Caesar Salad and pizza can be perfectly paired with pancakes too. Give it a try!

INGREDIENTS

One 2-ounce tin of oil-packed anchovies

1 tablespoon chopped fresh parsley

¼ cup cream cheese

½ teaspoon cayenne pepper

1 batch Yeast Pancakes (page 13), stacked on a plate and covered with a cloth

When making pancakes for savory dishes, remember to omit the sugar and vanilla.

PREPARATION

1. In food processor fitted with a metal blade, process the anchovies, parsley, cream cheese and cayenne pepper into smooth.

2. To serve, arrange the pancakes on individual serving dishes. Top with anchovy spread and serve immediately.

Ham 'n' Cheese Pancakes

Serves

4

Here's a tasty twist to a perennial favorite. Serve up gently heated slices of ham with flavorful corn pancakes and grated cheddar cheese. Serve with a tall glass of cold milk.

INGREDIENTS

½ pound ham, sliced into thin strips

1 batch Corn Pancakes (page 44), stacked on a plate and covered with a cloth

⅓ cup grated cheddar cheese

When making pancakes for savory dishes, remember to omit the sugar and vanilla.

PREPARATION

1. Heat a nonstick frying pan over medium heat. Add the ham slices and heat for about 30 seconds on each side.

2. To serve, arrange the pancakes on a serving dish. Top with the ham slices, sprinkle with cheese, and serve immediately.

Corn Pancakes

Serves

4

These hearty pancakes are fantastic at brunch. Serve on a bed of fresh parsley, with tangy sour cream or Greek-style yogurt on the side.

INGREDIENTS

⅔ cup heavy cream

1 clove garlic

3 tablespoons fresh chopped coriander

½ teaspoon fresh chopped chili pepper

1 cup + 1 cup frozen corn kernels

½ cup all-purpose white flour

1 teaspoon baking powder

½ teaspoon salt

2 large eggs

3 tablespoons melted butter, plus more for greasing

⅔ cup cold milk

When making pancakes for savory dishes, remember to omit the sugar and vanilla.

PREPARATION

1. In a food processor, process the cream, garlic, coriander, chili pepper and 1 cup of the corn for about 1 minute, until a smooth paste forms.

2. In a large bowl, sift together the flour, baking powder and salt.

3. Whisk the eggs and melted butter into the flour mixture, then gradually add the milk, stirring constantly until the batter is thick and smooth.

4. Mix in the cream mixture, then the remaining 1 cup of corn, stirring until evenly combined.

5. Cover the mixture with plastic wrap and let it rest for 30 minutes.

6. Heat a large nonstick frying pan over medium heat and brush with a thin coating of butter. Pour 2 or 3 tablespoons of batter onto the pan in three different places, leaving space between each pancake so that they do not stick together.

7. Cook until the bottom of the pancake is golden and there are bubbles on the surface of the pancake, a few of which have burst. Using a long thin spatula, flip each pancake and cook for another 1 or 2 minutes.

8. When the pancakes are golden on both sides, arrange in a stack on a large plate and cover with a clean cloth.

9. Repeat with the remaining batter. Serve immediately or store, covered with aluminum foil or parchment paper, for up to 20 minutes in a warm oven.

Pancakes with Bacon & Eggs

Serves

4

To prepare hard-boiled eggs that are easy to peel, simmer the eggs in boiling water for about 8 minutes and then immerse them in a bowl of cold water.

INGREDIENTS

½ pound bacon strips

¼ cup crème fraîche

½ teaspoon smoked Spanish paprika

1 batch Corn Pancakes (page 44), stacked on a plate and covered with a cloth

4 hard-boiled eggs, peeled and halved

When making pancakes for savory dishes, remember to omit the sugar and vanilla.

PREPARATION

1. Preheat the oven to 400°F and line a baking sheet with parchment paper.

2. Arrange the bacon strips on the baking sheet and bake for 7 to 8 minutes, until bacon is crispy and golden.

3. Combine the crème fraîche with paprika in a small bowl and set aside.

4. To serve, arrange the pancakes on a serving dish and add bacon and eggs. Serve with the crème fraîche mixture on the side.

Cream Cheese
& Salmon Pancakes

Serves

4

The combination of smoked salmon and cream cheese is always a hit at brunch. Replace traditional bagels with fresh pancakes and you have a fabulous twist on the same great flavors.

INGREDIENTS

¼ cup cream cheese

½ teaspoon smoked Spanish paprika

1 batch Multigrain Pancakes (page 16), stacked on a plate and covered with a cloth

½ pound smoked salmon

½ cup sunflower seed sprouts, for garnish

When making pancakes for savory dishes, remember to omit the sugar and vanilla.

PREPARATION

1. Combine the cream cheese and paprika in a small bowl and set aside.

2. To serve, arrange the pancakes on a serving dish.

3. Top each pancake with a bit of the cream cheese mixture and fold a piece of salmon on top.

4. Garnish with sunflower seed sprouts and serve.

Pancakes with Roquefort Cheese & Roasted Walnuts

Serves

4

Create an unusual sandwich featuring melted cheese, crunchy nuts, and nutty Multigrain pancakes. Try to make the pancakes identical in size, so it's easy to make tidy sandwiches with them.

INGREDIENTS

½ pound Roquefort cheese, crumbled

½ cup roasted walnuts, coarsely crushed

1 batch Multigrain Pancakes (page 16), stacked on a plate and covered with a cloth

When making pancakes for savory dishes, remember to omit the sugar and vanilla.

PREPARATION

1. In a medium bowl, combine the cheese and the walnuts.

2. To serve, spread some of the cheese mixture onto a pancake and place another pancake on top. Repeat with the rest of the pancakes and cheese mixture.

3. If you like, place the pancake sandwiches in a warm waffle iron for about 30 seconds, to melt the cheese before serving.

Pancakes with Spiced Corn & Grated Cheese

Serves

4

This flavorful dish is sure to attract interest. Spicy paprika, sweet corn and sharp cheddar all combine in a fragrant pancake dish.

INGREDIENTS

2 tablespoons softened butter, plus more for greasing

1 garlic clove, chopped

½ pound frozen corn kernels

1 teaspoon sweet paprika

½ teaspoon salt

½ teaspoon cayenne pepper

1 tablespoon chopped parsley

1 batch Yeast Pancakes (page 13), stacked on a plate and covered with a cloth

½ pound grated cheddar cheese

When making pancakes for savory dishes, remember to omit the sugar and vanilla.

PREPARATION

1. Preheat the oven to 400°F and lightly grease a baking tray.

2. In a frying pan, sauté the butter, garlic and corn over medium heat for about 3 minutes.

3. Add the paprika, salt, pepper and parsley, and sauté for another 3 minutes.

4. Remove from the heat and set aside.

5. Arrange the pancakes in overlapping rows on a baking tray. Distribute the corn mixture on top of the pancakes and then sprinkle the cheese on top.

6. Bake for 5 minutes or until cheese melts completely. Serve immediately.

Cream Cheese
& Caviar Pancakes

Serves

For this gorgeous recipe, I like making silver-dollar pancakes that are about 1 inch in diameter. The smaller size increases the elegance, making them a perfect finger food.

INGREDIENTS

1 batch Yeast Pancakes (page 13), stacked on a plate and covered with a cloth

½ pound cream cheese

¼ cup salmon caviar

When making pancakes for savory dishes, remember to omit the sugar and vanilla.

PREPARATION

1. Arrange the pancakes on a serving dish.

2. Spread cream cheese on each pancake and top with ½ teaspoon of caviar. Serve immediately.

Goat Cheese & Tapenade Pancakes

Serves

 4

Enjoy a Mediterranean medley of flavors with this dish. The rich olive paste harmonizes perfectly with the goat cheese, both in color and flavor.

INGREDIENTS

4 ounces pitted black olives

1 tablespoon chopped fresh parsley

1 garlic clove, crushed

½ teaspoon cayenne pepper

¼ cup olive oil, plus more for drizzling

1 batch Yeast Pancakes (page 13), stacked on a plate and covered with a cloth

12 ounces goat cheese, cut into slices

When making pancakes for savory dishes, remember to omit the sugar and vanilla.

PREPARATION

1. In a food processor fitted with a metal blade, combine the olives, parsley, garlic and cayenne pepper. Pulse until a smooth paste is formed.

2. Gradually add the olive oil between pulses until it is completely absorbed into the mixture.

3. To serve, top each pancake with a slice of cheese and a tablespoon of the olive paste.

4. Drizzle with olive oil and serve immediately.

Waffles

A Few Golden Rules

·

Basic Waffles
Basic Waffles Recipe 1
Basic Waffles Recipe 2
Basic Waffles Recipe 3
Belgian Waffles

·

Sweet Waffle Dishes
Banana Caramel Waffles
Tropical Waffles
Waffles with White Chocolate & Cherries
Latte Waffles
Apple Cinnamon Waffles with Ice Cream
Creamy Chocolate Waffles
Waffles with Cherries in Port
Waffles with Caramelized Pears
Waffles with Fresh Plum Jam
Pineapple & Piña Colada Waffles
Waffles with Fresh Custard & Berries
Citrus Sunrise Waffles
Waffles with Strawberries & Whipped Cream
Perfectly Pecan Waffles
Chocolate Crumble Waffle Sundae
Amaretto Peach Waffles
Waffles with Orange Custard & Ice Cream
Waffles with Buttery Baked Apricots

·

Savory Waffle Dishes
Waffles with Maple Beef Sauté
Waffles with Caramelized Orange Sauce & Turkey
Veal & Mushroom Stew with Waffles
Waffles with Teriyaki Chicken
Almond Shrimp Waffles
Waffles with Figs & Gorgonzola Cheese
Waffles with Saffron Salmon
Waffles with Goat Cheese & Tomato Confit
Herb & Nut Cream Cheese Waffles
Beef Ragout Waffles
Seafood Waffles au Gratin
Ratatouille Waffles
Waffles with Chicken in Mole Sauce

Waffles: A Few Golden Rules

Waffles are a wonderful dish to serve at brunch, as a comforting midday meal, or even as a light supper. Waffles leave lots of room for your imagination. They are fun to make and sure to attract compliments. In the coming pages, you'll find several basic waffle recipes. Try them out and find the one that works best for you—both in terms of ingredients and flavor—and turn it into your house favorite. Use it to make a variety of meals and desserts, simply by changing the toppings.

BAKING

• How you bake your waffles depends on the iron or griddle you're using, so read the manufacturer's instructions before you start. In many cases, you'll need to grease the iron with a bit of oil or butter first. Then ladle about ½ cup of batter onto the mold (again, this depends on the size of the waffle iron and the type of waffles you like) and smooth the top with a knife or spatula.

• Close the lid and bake until steam stops rising from the iron, then lift the lid and check the color of the waffle. If the color is too light, continue baking for another minute and then check again. A great waffle should be crispy on the outside, yet soft and tender on the inside.

EQUIPMENT

• Preparing waffles is easy, but you do need one key appliance: a waffle iron or griddle. These come in both stovetop and electrical varieties, as well as in diverse sizes and shapes. It may take a few attempts before you get your waffle iron to produce waffles just the way you like them, so be patient. All of the waffles in this book were made with electric waffle irons.

INGREDIENTS

• Read every recipe in advance, from start to finish, and make sure you have all the ingredients.

• For best results, use fresh butter, eggs and milk, and choose pure vanilla extract.

• Every basic waffle recipe makes about 4 to 6 waffles. The exact number depends on the size and thickness of your waffles. If you like thicker waffles, use more batter for each waffle; if you like thinner waffles, use less.

REHEATING & FREEZING

• Ideally, waffles should be served quite soon after baking. If you want to keep them warm while you prepare the topping, place them on a baking tray, cover with them with aluminum foil or parchment paper and store them in a warm oven until you're ready to serve.

• Waffles can also be reheated in the waffle iron. Just heat the iron for a few minutes, then turn the iron off, place the waffles inside and let them sit for about 1 minute.

• Waffles can be frozen for up to 1 week. If you plan on freezing waffles, first cool them to room temperature, then place them in an airtight container. Frozen waffles can be defrosted on the countertop or in the microwave.

SERVING

• Waffles are best served warm—the rest is really up to you. Use the photos in this book as inspiration and let your imagination lead the way. You can serve waffles flat on a plate and covered with sauce—all-time favorite—or cut them into cubes, slice them or halve them. Make the dish you serve as visually pleasing as it is tasty.

Basic Waffles Recipe 1

Serves

4

This basic recipe uses whipped eggs for volume and doesn't require any leavening agent. You don't need to wait for the batter to rise, which means it's a great recipe to make when you're short of time.

INGREDIENTS

1 cup all-purpose white flour

½ teaspoon salt

2 large eggs, separated

⅔ cup milk

¼ cup canola oil or melted butter

½ teaspoon vanilla extract

2 tablespoons sugar

PREPARATION

1. In a medium bowl, sift together the flour and salt.

2. In a separate bowl, combine the egg yolks, milk, oil and vanilla.

3. Form a hole in the middle of the dry ingredients and pour in the egg yolk mixture. Stir well until the batter is smooth.

4. In the bowl of an electric mixer, or using a hand mixer, beat the egg whites until soft and foamy. Slowly add the sugar, while beating, until stiff peaks form.

5. Gently fold the whipped egg whites into the batter, using a spatula.

6. The mixture can now be baked immediately or stored in the refrigerator for up to 1 hour.

7. To bake the waffles, heat your waffle iron and grease if necessary. Ladle about ½ cup of batter onto the mold (the exact quantity depends on your waffle iron) and smooth the top with a knife or spatula. Close the lid and bake until golden brown.

8. Transfer the waffles to a heatproof plate, cover with aluminum foil or parchment paper and keep in a warm oven until ready to serve.

Basic Waffles Recipe 2

This recipe includes baking powder as a leavening agent and can be made up to 3 hours in advance. The texture of the batter should be similar to mixed cake batter.

INGREDIENTS

1 cup all-purpose white flour

½ tablespoon baking powder

½ teaspoon salt

1 tablespoon sugar

2 large eggs, separated

⅔ cup milk

¼ cup canola oil or melted butter

½ teaspoon vanilla extract

PREPARATION

1. In a medium bowl, sift together the flour, baking powder, salt and sugar.

2. In a separate bowl, combine the egg yolks, milk, oil and vanilla.

3. Form a hole in the middle of the dry ingredients and pour in the egg yolk mixture. Stir well with a wood spoon until batter is smooth.

4. In a small bowl, using a hand mixer, whisk the egg whites until soft and foamy.

5. Gently fold the egg whites into the batter using a spatula.

6. The mixture can now be baked immediately or stored in the refrigerator for up to 3 hours.

7. To bake the waffles, heat your waffle iron and grease if necessary. Ladle about ½ cup of batter onto the mold (the exact quantity depends on your waffle iron) and smooth the top with a knife or spatula. Close the lid and bake until golden brown.

8. Transfer the waffle to a heatproof plate, cover with aluminum foil or parchment paper and keep in a warm oven until ready to serve.

Basic Waffles Recipe 3

4

This recipe uses fresh yeast as a leavening agent to produce a rich, satisfying waffle. It must be prepared well in advance, since the dough must first rest for 2 hours in the refrigerator and then rise for 1 hour on the counter.

INGREDIENTS

2 teaspoons fresh yeast

¼ cup cold milk

½ teaspoon vanilla extract

1 tablespoon brown sugar

1 cup all-purpose white flour

½ teaspoon salt

2 tablespoons softened butter

PREPARATION

1. In the bowl of a mixer fitted with the kneading hook, knead the yeast, milk, vanilla, brown sugar and flour on low speed for 3 minutes.

2. Add the salt and continue kneading on medium speed for 3 minutes.

3. Add the butter and knead on high speed for 5 minutes, or until the dough draws away from the sides of the bowl.

4. Transfer the dough to a floured bowl, cover it with plastic wrap and let it rest in the refrigerator for at least 2 hours (and no more than 24 hours).

5. Transfer the dough to a floured surface and cut into 4 even pieces. Roll each piece into a ball.

6. At this stage, the dough can be wrapped in plastic wrap and frozen for up to 1 week.

7. To prepare the waffles, place the pieces of dough on a floured surface and set aside to rise for 1 hour, until they double in size.

8. Heat your waffle iron and grease if necessary. Press one ball of dough onto the waffle mold. Close the lid and bake until golden brown.

9. Transfer the waffles to a heatproof plate, cover with aluminum foil or parchment paper and keep in a warm oven until ready to serve.

Belgian Waffles

4

This recipe creates a dark and delicious waffle that's satisfying and aromatic. Note that the batter in this recipe must rise for about 45 minutes before baking, so plan in advance. The batter should be a bit sticky and similar to mixed cake batter.

INGREDIENTS

⅔ cup milk, room temperature

1 teaspoon dry yeast

½ teaspoon vanilla extract

½ teaspoon brown sugar

½ teaspoon salt

1 cup all-purpose white flour

¼ cup melted butter

2 large egg whites

PREPARATION

1. In a medium bowl, combine the milk, yeast, vanilla, brown sugar, salt and flour with a wooden spoon for about 3 minutes, until a dough forms.

2. Pour in the butter and continue stirring for another 3 minutes. At this stage, the dough should have a smooth, uniform texture and be moist.

3. Cover the dough with a clean kitchen towel and let it rise in a warm place for 45 minutes.

4. About 5 minutes before the dough finishes rising, whisk the egg whites into a soft foam and gently fold into the dough, using a rubber spatula, until well blended.

5. The mixture can now be baked immediately or stored in the refrigerator for up to 3 hours.

6. To bake the waffles, heat your waffle iron and grease if necessary. Ladle about ½ cup of batter onto the mold (the exact quantity depends on your waffle iron) and smooth the top with a knife or spatula. Close the lid and bake until golden brown.

7. Transfer the waffles to a heatproof plate, cover with aluminum foil or parchment paper and keep in a warm oven until ready to serve.

Banana Caramel Waffles

4

This topping is a favorite among kids and adults alike. When making it for adults, soak the bananas in rum for 30 minutes first. Sprinkle on some coconut flakes for a taste of the tropics.

INGREDIENTS

¼ cup sugar

½ cup heavy cream

½ teaspoon pure vanilla extract

4 ripe bananas, cut into ¼-inch slices

1 batch waffles (pages 60-63), freshly baked, covered with foil and stored in an oven set at 200°F

PREPARATION

1. In a small saucepan, heat the sugar over medium heat until it turns a golden caramel color.

2. Add the cream, reduce the heat to low and continue cooking, stirring occasionally, until a thick caramel sauce forms.

3. Remove the cream from the heat, mix in the vanilla and set aside to cool for about 30 minutes.

4. In a nonstick frying pan over medium heat, sauté the bananas until golden on each side.

5. Remove the frying pan from the heat and gently stir in the caramel sauce.

6. To serve, cut the waffles into quarters and arrange in a stack on individual serving dishes. Serve each stack with some banana caramel mixture on the side and drizzle a bit on top too. Serve immediately.

Tropical Waffles

4

For best flavor, prepare the fruit salad in advance so the flavors have a chance to blend. Any of the fruit listed below can be replaced with another fruit that's in season. If the fruit you are using aren't quite ripe enough, mix in a bit of sugar.

INGREDIENTS

2 ripe bananas, cut into ¼-inch slices

1 fresh pineapple, peeled, cored and cut into ¼-inch dice

1 mango, peeled, pitted and cut into ¼-inch dice

6 passion fruit, cut in half with pulp removed

½ teaspoon pure vanilla extract

1 batch waffles (pages 60-63), freshly baked, covered with foil and stored in an oven set at 200°F

PREPARATION

1. In a medium bowl, combine the bananas, pineapple, mango, passion fruit and vanilla. Mix gently to combine and then set aside.

2. To serve, place each waffle on a serving dish and spoon the fruit mixture on top. Serve immediately.

Waffles with White Chocolate & Cherries

Serves

4

This beautiful dish features creamy white chocolate, bright red cherries, and fresh warm waffles. The topping is rich, so it's just right for serving with mini waffles.

INGREDIENTS

¼ cup heavy cream

1 teaspoon pure vanilla extract

6 ounces white chocolate, cut into chunks

1 batch waffles (pages 60-63), freshly baked, covered with foil and stored in an oven set at 200°F

½ pound fresh cherries, pitted

PREPARATION

1. In a small saucepan over medium heat, bring the cream and vanilla just to the boiling point.

2. Remove the cream from the heat and whisk in the chocolate until a smooth ganache forms.

3. To serve, arrange the waffles on individual serving dishes and top evenly with the cherries. Pour the chocolate ganache on top and serve.

Latte Waffles

4

Waffles are often served with a cup of warm coffee. In this dish, the coffee is right inside—with a dash of coffee liqueur for good measure.

INGREDIENTS

¼ cup sugar

½ cup heavy cream

1 tablespoon instant coffee

1 tablespoon coffee liqueur

1 batch waffles (pages 60-63), freshly baked, covered with foil and stored in an oven set at 200°F

8 scoops walnut ice cream

PREPARATION

1. In a small saucepan, heat the sugar over medium heat, until it turns a golden caramel color.

2. Reduce heat to low and mix in the cream and coffee.

3. Cook, stirring occasionally, until a thick caramel sauce forms.

4. Remove the mixture from the heat, mix in the liqueur and then set aside.

5. To serve, place 1 waffle on each serving dish.

6. Top with ice cream and pour the coffee sauce on top.

Apple Cinnamon Waffles with Ice Cream

Serves

4

This makes a delicious dessert on a crisp autumn day. The smell of apples baked in cinnamon, combined with the aroma of freshly baked waffles, will warm any heart—and every appetite!

INGREDIENTS

¼ cup butter

¼ cup sugar

6 Granny Smith apples, peeled, cored and cut into ¼-inch dice

1 teaspoon ground cinnamon or 4 cinnamon sticks

1 batch waffles (pages 60-63), freshly baked, covered with foil and stored in an oven set at 200°F

4 scoops vanilla ice cream

PREPARATION

1. In a large frying pan, heat the butter and sugar over medium heat until the sugar dissolves.

2. Mix in the apples and cinnamon and cook, stirring occasionally, for about 10 minutes until the apples are golden and soft.

3. Remove from the heat and set aside.

4. To serve, place 1 or 2 waffles on each serving dish.

5. Spoon an even amount of the apple mixture over each waffle and top with a scoop of ice cream.

6. Serve immediately.

Creamy Chocolate Waffles

Creamy Chocolate Waffles

Serves 4

Freshly baked waffles, warm chocolate syrup and rich vanilla ice cream—in a word, delicious! Use mini-waffles to make this dish—a perfect dessert.

INGREDIENTS

¾ cup heavy cream

2 tablespoons sugar

1 teaspoon pure vanilla extract

5 ounces dark chocolate, cut into small chunks

1 batch waffles (pages 60-63), freshly baked, covered with foil and stored in an oven set at 200°F

8 scoops vanilla ice cream

PREPARATION

1. In a small saucepan over medium heat, heat the cream, sugar and vanilla just until boiling.

2. As soon as the mixture boils, remove it from the heat and mix in the chocolate. Stir until mixture is thick and smooth and then set aside.

3. To serve, place 1 or 2 waffles on each serving dish. Top with 1 scoop of ice cream and pour warm chocolate sauce on top. Serve immediately.

Waffles with Cherries in Port

Serves 4

The sauce in this recipe thickens as it cools, so don't worry if it isn't quite thick enough when you remove it from the heat. Serve with mini waffles for a sophisticated yet simple dessert!

INGREDIENTS

½ pound frozen pitted cherries

2 tablespoons sugar

3 tablespoons port wine

½ teaspoon fresh lemon juice

1 batch waffles (pages 60-63), freshly baked, covered with foil and stored in an oven set at 200°F

PREPARATION

1. In a medium saucepan over medium heat, cook the cherries and sugar for about 10 minutes, until there is a fair amount of juice in the saucepan.

2. Reduce the heat to low heat, add the port and the lemon juice, and cook for 30 minutes, until the sauce is thick and dark. If the sauce isn't quite thick enough, cook for a few more minutes. Remove from the heat and set aside.

3. To serve, place 1 or 2 waffles on each serving dish. Top with a spoonful of cherries and pour the sauce over top. Serve immediately.

Waffles with Caramelized Pears

Serves

4

Maple syrup is a natural waffle condiment. In this mouth-watering variation, simmered pears are added as a sophisticated side dish. The pears can be sliced in half (as pictured) or cut into quarters.

INGREDIENTS

2 tablespoons butter

2 tablespoons brown sugar

4 Bosc pears, halved lengthwise

1 batch waffles (pages 60-63), freshly baked, covered with foil and stored in an oven set at 200°F

4 tablespoons maple syrup

PREPARATION

1. In a large frying pan, heat the butter and brown sugar over medium heat, until the sugar dissolves.

2. Add the pears and cook for about 10 minutes, stirring occasionally, until the pears are soft but still hold their shape. Remove from the heat and set aside.

3. To serve, cut each waffle in half and stack 4 halves on each serving dish. Serve with the pear halves on the side. Pour maple syrup on top.

Waffles with Fresh Plum Jam

Serves

4

Pistachios are an excellent nutty complement for the smooth sweetness of the plums. Substitute with crushed cashews or almonds if you like.

INGREDIENTS

¼ cup sugar

10 ripe purple plums, pitted and cut into ½-inch pieces

1 teaspoon lemon juice

1 batch waffles (pages 60-63), freshly baked, covered with foil and stored in an oven set at 200°F

1 tablespoon coarsely crushed pistachios, for garnish

PREPARATION

1. In a medium saucepan, heat the sugar over medium heat until it dissolves.

2. Reduce the heat to low heat, add the plums, and cook for 40 minutes, stirring occasionally, until a chunky jam forms.

3. Stir in the lemon juice, cook for another 2 minutes, then remove from the heat and set aside.

4. To serve, arrange the waffles on individual serving dishes and top with a spoonful of jam. Sprinkle crushed pistachios on top and serve.

Waffles with Caramelized Pears

Pineapple & Piña Colada Waffles

Serves

4

This refreshing recipe features fresh pineapple and whipped cream. Close your eyes, take a bite and imagine yourself on an all-inclusive cruise to the tropical islands.

INGREDIENTS

1 fresh pineapple, peeled, cored and cut into ½-inch dice

1 tablespoon + 2 tablespoons Piña Colada liquor

1 cup heavy cream

¼ cup powdered sugar

1 batch waffles (pages 60-63), freshly baked, covered with foil and stored in an oven set at 200°F

PREPARATION

1. Place the pineapple chunks in a bowl and pour 1 tablespoon of liquor on top. Mix gently so that the liquor coats all the pineapple chunks and then set aside.

2. In the bowl of an electric mixer, whip the cream and powdered sugar until stiff peaks form.

3. Using a whisk or rubber spatula, stir in the remaining 2 tablespoons of liquor.

4. To serve, place a waffle on an individual serving dish, top with the whipped cream and pineapples. Serve immediately.

Waffles with Fresh Custard & Berries

Serves

4

Berries, custard and waffles make a perfect Sunday morning breakfast in berry season. Use strawberries, blueberries or any other type of fresh berry.

INGREDIENTS

1 cup milk

1½ tablespoons + 1½ tablespoons sugar

1 teaspoon pure vanilla extract

4 large egg yolks

PREPARATION

1. In a medium saucepan over medium heat, bring the milk, 1½ tablespoons of sugar and vanilla to a boil.

2. In a separate bowl, using a hand mixer or whisk, whisk together the egg yolks, cornstarch and remaining 1½ tablespoons of sugar.

2 tablespoons cornstarch

1 batch waffles (pages 60-63), freshly baked, covered with foil and stored in an oven set at 200°F

½ pound fresh berries (strawberries, raspberries, blueberries)

1 tablespoon powdered sugar, for dusting

3. As soon as the milk mixture begins to boil, reduce the heat to low and whisk in the egg mixture.

4. Cook the mixture, whisking occasionally, until a thick custard forms.

5. Remove the custard from the heat and pour it into a clean bowl. Press a piece of plastic wrap against the surface to create an airtight seal and transfer it to the freezer. Chill for at least 45 minutes (and no more than 1 hour). At this stage, the custard may be refrigerated for up to 24 hours.

6. To serve, place a spoonful of custard onto each waffle, top generously with berries and dust with powdered sugar.

Citrus Sunrise Waffles

Serves

4

This refreshing dish can be served in the morning with a glass of fresh orange juice, or in the afternoon with fresh aromatic tea.

INGREDIENTS

4 fresh oranges

3 tablespoons sugar

1 batch waffles (pages 60-63), freshly baked, covered with foil and stored in an oven set at 200°F

4 scoops orange or lemon sorbet

PREPARATION

1. Cut the oranges (with rind) into quarters and remove the seeds. Transfer to a food processor fitted with a metal blade and pulse until a smooth paste forms.

2. In a medium saucepan, heat the sugar over medium heat, until it turns a light caramel color.

3. Add the processed oranges and cook over low heat for 30 to 40 minutes, until a thick jam forms. Remove from the heat and set aside.

4. To serve, place 1 waffle on each serving dish and top with a scoop of sorbet. Pour fresh orange jam on top and serve immediately.

Waffles with Strawberries & Whipped Cream

Serves

4

Strawberries are a natural topping to so many breakfast foods—and waffles are no exception. Add a few springs of fresh mint for an easy flavorful upgrade.

INGREDIENTS

½ pound fresh strawberries, cut into chunks

1 tablespoon granulated sugar

½ pound frozen mixed berries

½ teaspoon lemon juice

2 teaspoons + 2 teaspoons powdered sugar

1 cup heavy cream

1 batch waffles (pages 60-63), freshly baked, covered with foil and stored in an oven set at 200°F

1 tablespoon fresh mint leaves, for garnish

PREPARATION

1. In a medium bowl, gently combine the strawberries and granulated sugar. Refrigerate until ready to serve.

2. In a blender, combine the frozen berries, lemon juice and 2 teaspoons of powdered sugar. Blend until smooth. If you prefer a smoother sauce, pour it through a fine-mesh strainer and then set aside.

3. In the bowl of an electric mixer, beat the cream and the remaining 2 teaspoons of powdered sugar until stiff peaks form.

4. To serve, arrange the waffles on individual serving dishes. Spoon the whipped cream and fresh strawberries on top.

5. Garnish with a few mint leaves and serve with the berry sauce on the side.

Perfectly Pecan Waffles

Serves

4

Could anyone possibly resist a dessert made with freshly baked waffles, creamy ganache and crispy pecans? If the ganache hardens before you serve it, soften it by warming it in a heatproof bowl over a saucepan with gently simmering water.

INGREDIENTS

¼ cup pecan chunks

½ cup heavy cream

5 ounces semi-sweet chocolate, cut into small chunks

1 batch waffles (pages 60-63), freshly baked, covered with foil and stored in an oven set at 200°F

PREPARATION

1. In a dry pan over medium heat, gently toast the pecans, stirring with a wooden spoon until golden.

2. Remove from the heat and set aside to cool.

3. In a small saucepan over medium heat, heat the cream just to the boiling point.

4. Remove the cream from the heat and whisk in the chocolate, stirring until a smooth ganache forms. Stir in half of the pecans.

5. To serve, cut the waffles in half and arrange on individual serving dishes.

6. Drizzle the ganache over the top and sprinkle with the remaining pecans. Serve immediately.

Chocolate Crumble Waffle Sundae

4

Upgrade a standard ice cream sundae by incorporating a few cubes of freshly baked waffles. You can serve this dish as it appears in the photo, or place the waffle cubes below the ice cream and crumbs so that they can absorb the flavors.

INGREDIENTS

1 cup all-purpose white flour

½ cup sugar

2 tablespoons high-quality cocoa

½ cup softened butter

1 large egg

1 batch waffles (pages 60-63), freshly baked, covered with foil and stored in an oven set at 200°F

4 scoops maple ice cream

PREPARATION

1. Preheat the oven to 375°F and line a baking sheet with parchment paper.

2. On a clean work surface, pour the flour into a heap, then top with the sugar and cocoa. Mix the ingredients with your hands until uniformly combined.

3. Still using your fingers, mix in the butter until mixture is crumbly and moist, with a texture resembling wet sand.

4. Form a hole in the middle of the mixture and crack the egg into it. Continue mixing the mixture with your fingers until large crumbs form.

5. Using a spatula, pat the mixture in an even layer on the baking sheet.

6. Bake for about 20 minutes, until the chunks in the mixture are crispy.

7. Remove mixture from the oven and cool for about 30 minutes.

8. To serve, place 1 scoop of ice cream into each individual serving bowl. Top with even amounts of the crumble mixture and the cubed waffles. Serve immediately.

Amaretto Peach Waffles

Serves

4

Celebrate peaches when they're in season with this delightful recipe. If you like, replace the peaches with drained canned apricots and use half the amount of sugar.

INGREDIENTS

4 ripe peaches, pitted and cut into ½-inch chunks

1 tablespoon almond-flavored liqueur

1 tablespoon powdered sugar

1 batch waffles (pages 60-63), freshly baked, covered with foil and stored in an oven set at 200°F

4 scoops almond ice cream

PREPARATION

1. In a small bowl, combine the peaches, liqueur and powdered sugar. Refrigerate for 30 seconds.

2. To serve, place the waffles on individual dishes. Spoon the peach mixture on top and then add a scoop of ice cream. Serve immediately.

Waffles with Orange Custard & Ice Cream

Serves

4

Fresh orange crème is surprisingly easy to prepare and remarkable refreshing. Serve at breakfast with fresh yogurt and fragrant coffee.

INGREDIENTS

1 cup fresh orange juice

1½ tablespoons + 1½ tablespoons sugar

4 large egg yolks

2 tablespoons cornstarch

4 scoops almond ice cream

PREPARATION

1. In a medium saucepan over medium heat, bring the orange juice and 1½ tablespoons of sugar to a boil.

2. While the juice is heating, in a medium bowl, whisk together the egg yolks, cornstarch, and remaining 1½ tablespoons of sugar.

3. Once the orange juice comes to a boil, reduce the heat and whisk in the egg yolk mixture.

4. Cook the mixture, stirring occasionally, until a thick custard forms.

5. Remove the custard from the heat and pour it into a clean bowl.

6. Press a piece of plastic wrap against the surface to create an airtight seal and transfer it to the freezer.

7. Chill for at least 45 minutes (and no more than 1 hour). At this stage, the custard may be refrigerated for up to 24 hours.

8. To serve, arrange the waffles on individual serving dishes, and top each one with a spoonful of custard and a scoop of ice cream. Serve immediately.

Waffles with Buttery Baked Apricots

Serves

4

Crème fraîche is a rich, slightly sour cream that is an excellent topping for so many fresh pastries, including waffles. Served with fragrant baked apricots, this indulgence won't be easily forgotten.

INGREDIENTS

12 large fresh apricots, halved and pitted

2 tablespoons sugar

1 tablespoon melted butter

1 batch waffles (pages 60-63), freshly baked, covered with foil and stored in an oven set at 200°F

4 tablespoons crème fraîche

PREPARATION

1. Preheat the oven to 400°F. Arrange the apricot halves on a baking tray with high edges.

2. Sprinkle evenly with the sugar and then drizzle melted butter over top.

3. Bake for 15 to 20 minutes until golden.

4. To serve, place waffles on individual serving dishes.

5. Arrange 6 apricot halves on each waffle and drizzle with the juice from the baking tray.

6. Top each serving with a tablespoon of crème fraîche and serve immediately.

Waffles with Maple Beef Sauté

4

The sauce in this recipe will thicken a bit as it cools, so don't worry if it isn't quite thick enough when you remove it from the heat.

INGREDIENTS

1 pound beef steak, cut into 2-inch strips

¼ cup dry white wine

½ clove garlic, finely chopped

2 tablespoons maple syrup

½ teaspoon salt

½ teaspoon ground black pepper

2 tablespoons butter

1 batch waffles (pages 60-63), freshly baked, covered with foil and stored in an oven set at 200°F

When making waffles for savory dishes, remember to omit the sugar and vanilla.

PREPARATION

1. Heat a dry frying pan for about 5 minutes over medium heat until scorching.

2. Add the beef and sear until golden on each side.

3. Mix in the wine, garlic and maple syrup.

4. Cook, mixing occasionally, for about 5 minutes, until the sauce reduces by half.

5. Add the salt, pepper and butter and cook until sauce thickens a bit. Remove from the heat and set aside.

6. To serve, arrange the waffles on individual dishes, and top with the beef mixture. Serve immediately.

Waffles with Caramelized Orange Sauce & Turkey

Serves

4

This hearty dish features a range of flavors, including cayenne pepper, zesty orange juice and hearty waffles. Serve with a cold beer for a hearty snack on a weekend afternoon.

INGREDIENTS

1 pound turkey breast, cut into 2-inch strips

½ teaspoon salt

½ teaspoon ground black pepper

1 tablespoon brown sugar

½ cup freshly squeezed orange juice

½ teaspoon cayenne pepper

½ teaspoon dried oregano

2 tablespoons butter

1 batch waffles (pages 60-63), freshly baked, covered with foil and stored in an oven set at 200°F

Fresh oregano, for garnish

When making waffles for savory dishes, remember to omit the sugar and vanilla.

PREPARATION

1. Heat a dry frying pan for about 5 minutes over medium heat until scorching.

2. Add the turkey, salt and pepper and sear until the turkey is brown on all sides.

3. Remove the turkey from the pan and set aside.

4. Add brown sugar to the frying pan and cook, stirring occasionally, until a brown caramel forms. Mix in the orange juice, add the pepper and oregano and cook, mixing occasionally, until the sauce reduces by half.

5. Return the turkey to the frying pan, add the butter and cook, until the sauce thickens a bit. Remove from the heat and set aside.

6. To serve, cut the waffles in half and arrange on individual serving dishes.

7. Top with the turkey and orange sauce and garnish with fresh oregano. Serve immediately.

Veal & Mushroom Stew with Waffles

Serves

Surprise guests with the interesting combination of ingredients in this dish: wild mushrooms, tender veal and fragrant homemade waffles.

INGREDIENTS

1 pound veal shoulder, cut into ½-inch dice

½ teaspoon salt

½ teaspoon cayenne pepper

½ cooking onion, finely sliced

1 tablespoon butter

1 clove garlic, chopped

½ pound wild mushrooms (such as shiitake, cremini or oyster)

1 tablespoon dried Porcini mushrooms, chopped

¼ cup dry white wine

½ cup heavy cream

1 batch waffles (pages 60-63), freshly baked, covered with foil and stored in an oven set at 200°F

Fresh oregano, for garnish

When making waffles for savory dishes, remember to omit the sugar and vanilla.

PREPARATION

1. Heat a dry frying pan over medium heat for about 5 minutes until scorching.

2. Add the veal, salt and pepper. Cook while stirring until veal is golden. Remove the veal from the pan and set aside.

3. Add the onion and butter to the frying pan and sauté until golden. Mix in the garlic and all the mushrooms and cook for 3 minutes, stirring occasionally, until mushrooms soften a bit.

4. Pour in the wine, return the veal to the pan and continue cooking, stirring occasionally, until the sauce reduces by half.

5. Mix in the cream and cook until the sauce thickens. Remove from heat and set aside.

6. To serve, arrange the waffles on individual serving dishes. Top with the veal stew, garnish with oregano and serve immediately.

Waffles with Teriyaki Chicken

Serves 4

In this dish, you'll replace the rice from a traditional Asian style meal with savory waffles. Surprising and satisfying.

INGREDIENTS

1 tablespoon sesame oil

1 clove garlic, crushed

1 teaspoon finely chopped fresh ginger

1 pound chicken breast, cut into ½-inch dice

3 tablespoons teriyaki sauce

1 batch waffles (pages 60-63), freshly baked, covered with foil and stored in an oven set at 200°F

¼ cup finely chopped green onions, for garnish

When making waffles for savory dishes, remember to omit the sugar and vanilla.

PREPARATION

1. Heat a frying pan over medium heat. Add the sesame oil, garlic and ginger, and sauté for 2 minutes, stirring occasionally.

2. Add the chicken and sauté until golden and cooked through. Pour in the teriyaki sauce, reduce the heat to low, and cook for another 5 minutes.

3. To serve, arrange the waffles on a serving platter and top with the teriyaki chicken. Garnish with green onions and serve immediately.

Almond Shrimp Waffles

Serves 4

This delicious dish features an irresistible combination of seafood and seasonings. You can almost smell the sea when you serve it.

INGREDIENTS

2 tablespoons olive oil

1 clove garlic, crushed

1 tablespoon finely chopped sun-dried tomatoes

PREPARATION

1. Heat a frying pan over medium heat. Add the oil and garlic and sauté for 2 minutes, stirring occasionally.

2. Mix in the dried tomatoes and almonds and cook for another 2 minutes, stirring occasionally.

¼ cup finely ground blanched almonds

½ cup tomato juice

½ teaspoon salt

½ teaspoon smoked Spanish paprika

1 pound fresh shrimp, cleaned, peeled, and cut lengthwise

1 batch waffles (pages 60-63), freshly baked, covered with foil and stored in an oven set at 200°F

When making waffles for savory dishes, remember to omit the sugar and vanilla.

3. Add the tomato juice, salt and paprika, and cook until the sauce thickens a bit.

4. Mix in the shrimp and cook for another 2 minutes, or until shrimp is cooked through.

5. To serve, arrange the waffles on a serving platter and top with the shrimp mixture.

Waffles with Figs & Gorgonzola Cheese

Serves

4

This fantastic dish features sweet fresh figs and salty gorgonzola cheese. Serve only when fresh figs are in season.

INGREDIENTS

12 ripe fresh figs, halved

2 teaspoons balsamic vinegar

1 tablespoon brown sugar

1 batch waffles (pages 60-63), freshly baked, covered with foil and stored in an oven set at 200°F

4 ounces gorgonzola cheese

When making waffles for savory dishes, remember to omit the sugar and vanilla.

PREPARATION

1. Preheat the oven to 400°F.

2. Place the figs in a small bowl and pour in the balsamic vinegar. Stir lightly, taking care not to damage the fruit, until the figs are coated.

3. Arrange the figs in a deep baking tray, cut side facing upward, and sprinkle with sugar. Bake for 10 minutes, then set aside to cool.

4. To serve, arrange the waffles on a serving dish and top with the figs. Crumble some cheese gorgonzola on top, and serve.

Waffles with Saffron Salmon

Serves

4

*Saffron is a cherished spice that's beautiful, fragrant and delicious.
Make the most of just a few strands with this lovely dish.*

INGREDIENTS

1 tablespoon butter

½ clove garlic, crushed

½ cup dry white wine

¼ teaspoon saffron

½ teaspoon salt

½ teaspoon cayenne pepper

¼ cup heavy cream

1 pound salmon filet, cut into 2-inch strips

1 teaspoon fresh lemon juice

1 batch waffles (pages 60-63), freshly baked, covered with foil and stored in an oven set at 200°F

Fresh thyme, for garnish

When making pancakes for savory dishes, remember to omit the sugar and vanilla.

PREPARATION

1. In a frying pan, melt the butter over medium heat. Add the garlic and sauté for 2 minutes.

2. Mix in the wine, saffron, salt and pepper. Cook until sauce reduces by half.

3. Add the cream and cook for about 6 to 8 minutes, until the sauce thickens.

4. Add the salmon and lemon juice and cook until salmon turns golden. Remove from the heat and set aside.

5. To serve, arrange the waffles on serving dishes and top with the salmon sauce.

6. Garnish with thyme and serve immediately.

Waffles with Goat Cheese & Tomato Confit

Serves

4

This impressive dish combines waffles with the elegance of homemade confit. Full of flavor and color!

INGREDIENTS

8 plum tomatoes, peeled, seeded and cut into quarters

1 head garlic cloves, peeled

½ cup olive oil

½ teaspoon sea salt

½ teaspoon ground black pepper

1 batch waffles (pages 60-63), freshly baked, covered with foil and stored in an oven set at 200°F

6 ounces ripe goat cheese, cut into ½-inch rounds

When making waffles for savory dishes, remember to omit the sugar and vanilla.

PREPARATION

1. Preheat the oven to 250°F.

2. In a baking dish, combine the tomatoes and garlic cloves. Toss with the olive oil, salt and pepper until evenly coated.

3. Bake for about 1 hour, until the garlic is very soft.

4. Let the mixture cool to room temperature, then transfer to a serving dish.

5. To serve, arrange the waffles on individual serving dishes and top with the cheese and homemade confit.

Herb & Nut Cream Cheese Waffles

Serves

4

Crunchy nuts, smooth cream cheese and aromatic waffles—the description alone makes you want a second helping! This topping is a cinch to make—and it goes so quickly that you should consider making a double batch.

INGREDIENTS

1 cup cream cheese

½ cup walnuts

2 tablespoons chopped fresh parsley

1 tablespoon chopped fresh basil

1 clove garlic, crushed

1 tablespoon fresh thyme leaves

½ teaspoon salt

½ teaspoon cayenne pepper

1 batch waffles (pages 60-63), freshly baked, covered with foil and stored in an oven set at 200°F

8 large cherry tomatoes, halved

When making waffles for savory dishes, remember to omit the sugar and vanilla.

PREPARATION

1. In a food processor fitted with a metal blade, combine the cream cheese, walnuts, parsley, basil, garlic, thyme, salt and pepper, until evenly combined but still chunky.

2. To serve, top each waffle with a thick layer of the cheese mixture.

3. Squeeze the cherry tomato halves on top to add color and flavor, and serve.

Beef Ragout Waffles

Serves

4

I recommend using canned Italian tomatoes to make this hearty dish, since they are naturally sweet and cook beautifully.

INGREDIENTS

1 carrot

1 cooking onion

1 celery stalk

2 garlic cloves

2 tablespoons olive oil

1 pound ground beef

1 teaspoon salt

½ teaspoon black pepper

1 teaspoon dried oregano

One 16-ounce can of peeled Italian tomatoes

1 batch waffles (pages 60-63), freshly baked, covered with foil and stored in an oven set at 200°F

When making waffles for savory dishes, remember to omit the sugar and vanilla.

PREPARATION

1. Preheat the oven to 400°F.

2. In a food processor fitted with a metal blade, process the carrot, onion, celery and garlic until ground.

3. In a saucepan over medium heat, cook the olive oil, beef and vegetable mixture for about 5 minutes, stirring occasionally.

4. Add the salt, pepper, oregano and tomatoes, and continue cooking until the mixture comes to a boil.

5. Remove from the heat, transfer to a heatproof baking dish and bake for 20 minutes.

6. To serve, place waffles on individual serving dishes and top with a spoonful of hot stew. Serve immediately.

Seafood Waffles au Gratin

4

This cheesy dish is perfect for serving when good friends come to visit. Hearty and heartwarming, it makes for a lovely winter lunch. Serve with a full-bodied red wine.

INGREDIENTS

1 pound precooked seafood

¼ cup heavy cream

1 teaspoon seafood seasoning, such as Old Bay

½ teaspoon salt

½ teaspoon cayenne pepper

1 batch waffles (pages 60-63), freshly baked, covered with foil and stored in an oven set at 200°F

1 cup grated Emmental cheese

When making waffles for savory dishes, remember to omit the sugar and vanilla.

PREPARATION

1. Preheat the oven to 400°F.

2. In a large bowl, combine the seafood, cream, seasoning, salt, and cayenne pepper. Chill for at least 15 minutes (and no more than 1 hour).

3. To serve, arrange the waffles on a baking sheet and distribute the seafood mixture evenly on top.

4. Sprinkle with cheese and bake for 12 to 15 minutes, until cheese is melted and golden. Serve immediately.

Ratatouille Waffles

Serves

4

Waffles may be an inherently North American dish, but they are excellent at adapting to international flavors. In this version they adopt a Mediterranean flavor.

INGREDIENTS

⅛ cup + ⅛ cup olive oil

2 carrots, cut into ¼-inch dice

1 zucchini, cut into ¼-inch dice

1 red pepper, seeded and cut into ¼-inch dice

1 eggplant, cut into ¼-inch dice

1 clove garlic, crushed

½ cup tomato juice

1 teaspoon salt

½ teaspoon ground black pepper

1 teaspoon finely chopped fresh thyme leaves

1 batch waffles (pages 60-63), freshly baked, covered with foil and stored in an oven set at 200°F

¼ pound feta cheese, crumbled

Fresh arugula leaves optional

When making waffles for savory dishes, remember to omit the sugar and vanilla.

PREPARATION

1. In a large frying pan, heat ⅛ cup of oil over medium heat. Add the carrots and sauté until golden.

2. Place a colander over a bowl. Using a slotted spoon, transfer the carrots from the pan to the colander.

3. Place the zucchini in the frying pan and sauté until golden. Transfer the zucchini to the colander containing the carrots, using a slotted spoon.

4. Sauté the red pepper next, then add to the colander.

5. Add the remaining ⅛ cup of oil to the frying pan, as well as the oil that drained off the carrots and zucchini. Mix in the eggplant and sauté until golden.

6. With the slotted spoon, transfer the eggplant to the colander and let it sit for a few moments to drain.

7. Discard the oil remaining in the frying pan and wipe the pan clean with a paper towel. Transfer the vegetables from the colander to the pan, add the garlic and sauté for about 1 minute.

8. Mix in the tomato juice, salt, pepper and thyme. Cook over low heat for 3 minutes, stirring occasionally.

9. To serve, arrange the waffles on individual serving dishes. Distribute the vegetable mixture evenly on top and sprinkle with feta cheese. Serve with fresh arugula leaves on the side.

Waffles with Chicken in Mole Sauce

Serves

4

Take your waffles on a Mexican adventure with this delicious recipe. If you've never tasted Mole sauce before, this is a great opportunity to try out this rich and distinct sauce.

INGREDIENTS

1 pound chicken breast, cut into 2-inch strips

1 tablespoon canola oil

3 tablespoons Mexican mole sauce

½ teaspoon salt

½ teaspoon cayenne pepper

1 batch waffles (pages 60-63), freshly baked, covered with foil and stored in an oven set at 200°F

1 chili pepper, seeded and sliced into thin rings, for garnish

---

When making waffles for savory dishes, remember to omit the sugar and vanilla.

PREPARATION

1. Preheat the oven to 375°F.

2. Arrange the chicken in a deep baking dish and cover with oil, mole sauce, salt and pepper. Stir to coat the chicken, then cover with aluminum foil and bake for about 20 minutes.

3. Remove the foil and bake for another 15 minutes, until chicken is cooked through.

4. To serve, arrange the waffles on individual serving dishes and top with slices of chicken. Pour over the sauce from the baking dish, garnish with chili pepper and serve.

Crêpes

A Few Golden Rules

•

Basic Crêpes
Basic Crêpes Recipe
Yorkshire Pudding Crêpes
Chestnut Flour (Necci) Crêpes

•

Sweet Crêpes Dishes
Apple & Cinnamon Crêpes
Crêpes with Pears in Port Wine
Ricotta & Honey Crêpes
Crêpes with Chocolate Raspberry Mousse
Cannoli di Palermo
Crêpes Normandy with Sweet Apples
Mille Feuilles Crêpes
Crêpes Suzette
Choco Hazelnut Cream Crêpes

•

Savory Crêpes Dishes
Mixed Seafood Crêpes
Rich Ratatouille Crêpes
Assorted Cheese Crêpes
Mushroom & Herb Crêpes
Ceviche Crêpes with Crème Fraîche
Anchovy & Dried Tomato Crêpes
Savory Herb Crêpes
Roasted Chicken & Corn Crêpes
Chili Con Carne Crêpes

Crêpes: A Few Golden Rules

Crêpes whisper elegance with every mouthful. They are light, tasty, impressive and versatile. Crêpes conjure up images of fine breakfasts in fancy cafes, but in truth they are really quite easy to make at home. All you need is a few basic ingredients and some essential equipment.

COOKING

• Make sure the pan you'll be cooking with is thoroughly heated before greasing.

• Brush the pan with butter or oil once it is warm. Using a small ladle, pour about 3 tablespoons of batter into the pan. Use the back of the ladle to spread the batter in a circular motion, from the middle to the edges, so that the mixture covers the pan evenly.

• Cook the crêpe for about 2 to 3 minutes, or until the edges draw away from the sides of the pan and the top is moist but not runny. Insert an offset spatula under the crêpe and check that the bottom is light golden.

• Flip over the crêpe and cook on the other side for another 2 to 3 minutes. When the bottom is a light golden color, transfer to a large plate and cover with a clean cloth.

• Keep a close eye on your crêpes as they cook, since it is easy to overcook them, which makes them dry and tasteless.

• When flipping crêpes, make sure the spatula reaches the center of the crêpe before flipping.

• I usually prepare the crêpes before I prepare the sauce or topping. I pile them onto a plate and cover them with a clean kitchen towel to keep them moist and fresh until I'm ready to serve them.

EQUIPMENT

A few essentials are important for making delicious crêpes:

Sifter Use this to sift the flour and baking powder for batter that is airy and lump-free. If you don't have a sifter, use a fine-mesh colander.

Hand mixer, whisk or electric mixer Use one of these to whisk the batter until light and smooth.

Flat crêpe pan or nonstick (ceramic or silicon-coated) skillet with low sides and a thick bottom Use either of these to cook great crêpes.

Small ladle Use this to transfer the batter to the pan.

Offset spatula This long, thin metallic spatula is perfect for flipping crêpes with ease.

INGREDIENTS

• Read every recipe in advance, from start to finish, and make sure you have all the ingredients.

• For best results, use fresh butter, eggs and milk and choose pure vanilla extract.

• Combine the liquids first and then add the dry ingredients, using a sifter.

• Every recipe in this book produces about eight 12-inch crêpes. Of course, the quantity and size of crêpes you make depends on the size of your pan.

• Crêpe batter can be refrigerated in an airtight container for up to 24 hours before cooking. This is a great advantage when preparing them for a party.

REHEATING & FREEZING

• Crêpes can be prepared up to 24 hours in advance. Store them in the refrigerator, wrapped in a clean towel, until ready to serve. Reheat them in a warm crêpe pan or microwave.

SERVING

• One of my favorite things about crêpes is the wonderful variety of ways in which they can be assembled. You can place a crêpe flat on a plate and simply drizzle sauce on top. You can also fold the crêpe over the size, in half or in quarters to create a tidy little envelope. Crêpes can also be rolled tightly, rolled loosely, stacked or sliced— whatever you like. The choice is really up to you, so use the images in this chapter as guidelines and let your imagination do the rest!

Basic Crêpes Recipe

Serves

 8

For an even richer result, substitute half of the milk for heavy cream. The outcome will be wonderful, but note that the crêpe will cook a bit faster.

INGREDIENTS

2 large eggs

2 tablespoons melted butter, plus more for greasing

1 cup cold milk

Pinch of salt

½ teaspoon vanilla extract

1 cup all-purpose white flour

2 tablespoons powdered sugar

PREPARATION

1. In a large bowl, mix the eggs, melted butter, milk, salt and vanilla.

2. Sift in the flour and powdered sugar. Stir until the batter is thick and smooth.

3. Cover with plastic wrap and refrigerate for at least 1 hour.

4. Heat a large crêpe pan over medium heat. Brush the pan with butter once it is warm.

5. Using a small ladle, pour about 3 tablespoons of batter into the pan. Use the back of the ladle to spread the batter in a circular motion, from the middle to the edges, so that the mixture covers the pan evenly.

6. Cook the crêpe for about 2 to 3 minutes, or until the edges draw away from the sides of the pan and the top is moist but not runny. Insert an offset spatula under the crêpe and check that the bottom is a light golden color.

7. Flip over the crêpe and cook on the other side for another 2 to 3 minutes, until light gold. Transfer the crêpe to a large plate and cover with a clean cloth.

8. Repeat with the remaining batter. Serve immediately or store, covered with a clean cloth, until ready to serve.

Yorkshire Pudding Crêpes

8

This hearty version is perfectly topped with gravy. For a really unique dish, prepare this batter in a muffin pan. Use a small ladle to distribute the batter, since you'll want to do it as quickly as possible.

INGREDIENTS

4 large eggs

¾ cup milk

½ teaspoon salt

1½ cups all-purpose white flour

2 tablespoons butter, for greasing

2 tablespoons cold water

PREPARATION

1. In the bowl of an electric mixer fitted with the whisk attachment, beat the eggs, milk and salt at medium speed for 2 minutes.

2. Sift in the flour and beat for 2 minutes, until the mixture is smooth.

3. Scrape down the sides of the bowl, then cover with plastic wrap and let it rest in the refrigerator for 2 hours.

4. About 30 minutes before the rest is completed, heat the oven to 450°F.

5. Put a bit of butter into each hole of a 12-hole muffin pan. Place the pan in the oven for about 2 minutes, or until the pan starts emitting a bit of smoke. Don't let the pan stay any longer, as the butter will start to burn.

6. In the meantime, mix the cold water into the batter and then pour the batter through a fine-mesh colander into a large bowl. (This helps remove any lumps that may have formed in the batter.)

7. Remove the muffin pan with the smoking butter and quickly spoon the batter into each muffin hole.

8. Reduce the oven heat to 400°F and bake for about 15 minutes or until golden brown. Serve immediately.

Chestnut Flour (Necci) Crêpes

Serves

8

This Italian recipe produces delicious gluten-free crêpes. Watch the crêpes closely as they cook, since they cook quite quickly. Even a few seconds of overcooking will cause them to be dry.

INGREDIENTS

1 large egg

1 tablespoon melted butter, plus more for greasing

¾ cup cold milk

Pinch of salt

1 cup chestnut flour

2 tablespoons powdered sugar

PREPARATION

1. In a large bowl, mix the egg, melted butter, milk and salt.

2. Sift the chestnut flour and powdered sugar into the bowl with the egg mixture. Stir until the batter is thick and smooth.

3. Cover with plastic wrap and refrigerate for at least 1 hour.

4. Heat a large crêpe pan over medium heat. Brush the pan with butter once it is warm.

5. Using a small ladle, pour about 3 tablespoons of batter into the pan. Use the back of the ladle to spread the batter in a circular motion, from the middle to the edges, so that the mixture covers the pan evenly.

6. Cook the crêpe for about 1 minute, until the edges draw away from the sides of the pan and the top is moist but not runny. Insert an offset spatula under the crêpe and check that the bottom is a light golden color.

7. Flip over the crêpe and cook on the other side until the bottom is light gold. Transfer the crêpe to a large plate and cover with a clean cloth.

8. Repeat with the remaining batter. Serve immediately or store, covered with a clean cloth, until ready to serve.

Apple & Cinnamon Crêpes

Serves

4

This is a fragrant favorite in my house. Warm, 'cinnamony' and delicious, it can be served at breakfast, as dessert, or with tea or coffee in the afternoon.

INGREDIENTS

3 tablespoons butter

⅓ cup white sugar

8 Granny Smith apples, peeled, cored and cut into slices

1 teaspoon cinnamon or 4 cinnamon sticks

1 batch crêpes (page 108), cooked, stacked and covered with a kitchen cloth

PREPARATION

1. Preheat the oven to 375°F.

2. In a large saucepan over medium heat, heat the butter and sugar until the sugar dissolves.

3. Mix in the apples and cinnamon and cook over medium heat, stirring constantly, for about 5 minutes.

4. Remove the apples from the heat, transfer to a deep baking sheet and bake for 20 minutes.

5. Arrange the crêpes in individual serving dishes. Top each one with baked apples and pour in the sauce from the baking sheet.

6. Serve immediately.

Crêpes with Pears in Port Wine

This is a great dessert to serve when entertaining. The filling can be prepared a day in advance, freeing you up for your other preparations before your guests arrive.

INGREDIENTS

4 Bartlett pears, peeled and halved lengthwise

1 cup port wine

2 tablespoons sugar

1 cinnamon stick

2 star anise

1 batch crêpes (page 108), cooked, stacked and covered with a kitchen cloth

PREPARATION

1. In a small saucepan over medium heat, bring the pears, port, sugar, cinnamon and star anise to a boil.

2. Reduce the heat to low and cook for about 10 minutes, until the pears are cooked but still firm.

3. Using a slotted spoon, remove the pears from the saucepan and set aside.

4. Continue cooking the port mixture for about 15 minutes, stirring occasionally, until a thick sauce forms.

5. Remove the sauce from the heat and set aside.

6. To serve, place 2 crêpes on each serving dish, top each crêpe with a pear half and pour sauce over the top.

7. Serve immediately.

Ricotta & Honey Crêpes

Serves

4

Who says crêpes have to be complicated? This dish is simple, natural, wholesome and delicious. You only need a few ingredients, so make sure the ones you choose are of a high quality.

INGREDIENTS

1 batch crêpes (page 108), cooked, stacked and covered in a clean kitchen cloth

4 tablespoons honey

1 cup ricotta cheese

PREPARATION

1. Place a crêpe on a serving dish and crumble some ricotta cheese on top. Drizzle with honey.

2. Fold the crêpe in half and then again in quarters, to form a wedge shape.

3. Repeat to create ricotta-filled wedges with all the crêpes. Serve immediately.

Crêpes with Chocolate Raspberry Mousse

Serves

4

INGREDIENTS

6 ounces unsweetened chocolate, cut into chunks

1 cup heavy cream

¼ cup sugar

½ cup fresh raspberries

1 batch crêpes (page 108), cooked, stacked and covered in a clean kitchen cloth

1 tablespoon powdered sugar, for decoration

PREPARATION

1. Using a double-boiler, or a medium bowl set over a pot of simmering water, melt the chocolate until smooth.

2. While the chocolate is melting, pour the cream into the bowl of an electric mixer and beat at high speed until the texture is soft and foamy. Add the sugar and continue beating until stiff peaks forms.

3. Remove the chocolate from the heat and mix until smooth. Add one-third of the whipped cream mixture to the melted chocolate and whisk together until smooth.

4. Fold the rest of the whipped cream into the chocolate cream mixture, folding until a light and smooth mousse forms. Carefully fold in the raspberries.

5. To serve, place 1 crêpe on a serving dish, top with 2 tablespoons of raspberry mousse, and sprinkle with sugar.

6. Repeat the process with the rest of the crêpes, and serve immediately.

Ricotta & Honey Crêpes

Cannoli di Palermo

This is a crêpe-based version of the traditional Sicilian recipe. It features a rich cream filling and delicious wine-enhanced crêpe batter. Impressive, indulgent and infused with the tastes of Italy! If you like, prepare the batter up to 1 day in advance.

INGREDIENTS

Cannoli

2 large eggs

2 tablespoons melted butter, plus more for greasing

Pinch of salt

¾ cup sweet red wine, such as Marsala

1 cup all-purpose white flour

½ teaspoon baking powder

1 tablespoon powdered sugar

Filling

1 pound fresh ricotta cheese

½ cup powdered sugar, plus more for decorating

⅓ cup light raisins

2 tablespoons sweet red wine, such as Marsala

PREPARATION

1. Prepare the cannoli: In a large bowl, mix the eggs, melted butter, salt and wine.

2. Sift in the flour, baking powder and powdered sugar. Whisk together until batter is thick and smooth.

3. Cover with plastic wrap and refrigerate for at least 1 hour, and up to 24 hours.

4. Heat a large crêpe pan over medium heat. Brush the pan with butter once it is warm.

5. Using a small ladle, pour about 3 tablespoons of batter into the pan. Use the back of the ladle to spread the batter in a circular motion, from the middle to the edges, so that the mixture covers the pan evenly.

6. Cook the crêpe for about 2 to 3 minutes, or until the edges draw away from the sides of the pan and the top is moist but not runny. Insert an offset spatula under the crêpe and check that the bottom is a light golden color.

7. Flip over the crêpe and cook on the other side for another 2 to 3 minutes, until light gold. Transfer the crêpe to a large plate and cover with a clean cloth.

8. Repeat with the remaining batter. Cover with a clean cloth until ready to serve.

9. Prepare the filling: In a large bowl, gently mix the cheese and powdered sugar until combined.

10. Fold in the raisins and wine until evenly combined. Make sure that you fold the mixture (rather than stir it) in order to preserve the texture of the cheese.

11. To serve, place 1 crêpe on your work surface and spread a wide strip of the cheese on the lower third of the crêpe. Roll up that end of the crêpe to form a cylinder. Repeat this process with the rest of the crêpes. Arrange on a serving dish, sprinkle with powdered sugar and serve.

Crêpes Normandy with Sweet Apples

Serves

4

Pamper your guests with an indulgent dessert of fresh crêpes, gently cooked apples, and a dash of brandy.

INGREDIENTS

8 Granny Smith apples, peeled, cored, and thinly sliced

⅓ cup powdered sugar, plus more for decoration

½ cup apple cider

3 teaspoons cold butter

½ tablespoon apple brandy liqueur, optional

1 batch crêpes (page 108), cooked, stacked, and covered with a kitchen cloth

PREPARATION

1. Heat a large saucepan over medium heat. Add the apples and powdered sugar and cook for about 10 minutes, stirring occasionally, until apples are soft and golden.

2. Using a slotted spoon, remove the apples from saucepan and set aside.

3. Return the saucepan to the heat, pour in the cider, and cook until the mixture reduces by half.

4. Add the butter and brandy and cook until the sauce thickens a bit. Remove from the heat and gently mix in the apples.

5. To serve, place a crêpe on a serving dish and top with a spoonful of the apple mixture. Fold the crêpe in half, add another spoonful of the apple mixture, then fold the crêpe into quarters. Repeat to fill all the crêpes, and serve immediately.

Mille Feuilles Crêpes

Serves

This gorgeous dessert features individual stacks of 4-inch crêpes alternating with fresh pastry cream. I use a 5-inch crêpe pan to make the crêpes and a pastry bag fitted with a 1/3-inch round tip to create the delicious balls of pastry cream.

INGREDIENTS

2 cups milk

5 large egg yolks

½ cup white sugar

2 tablespoons corn starch

1 teaspoon vanilla extract

½ cup cream cheese

1 batch crêpes (page 108), prepared in a 5-inch crêpe pan, stacked and covered with a clean kitchen cloth

Powdered sugar, for dusting

PREPARATION

1. In a medium saucepan over medium heat, bring the milk just to a boil.

2. Separately, in a small bowl, whisk together the egg yolks, sugar and corn starch.

3. As soon as the milk reaches the boiling point, mix in the vanilla and remove from the heat.

4. Pour half of the milk mixture into the egg yolk mixture, stirring continuously, until combined.

5. Pour the milk and egg mixture back into the saucepan and continue cooking over low heat, stirring constantly, until the mixture begins to bubble and thicken.

6. Cook for another minute while mixing, and then remove from the heat.

7. Pour the pastry cream into a clean bowl, cover with plastic wrap and refrigerate for about 1 hour. At this stage, the pastry cream may be refrigerated for up to 2 days.

8. Before serving, whisk the cream cheese into the pastry cream until smooth. Then transfer the mixture to a pastry bag with a ⅓-inch round tip.

9. Cut the crêpes, using a 4-inch round ring.

10. To serve, place 1 crêpe on a serving dish. Pipe dollops of the cream mixture onto the crêpe, then top with another crêpe and pipe more cream mixture on top.

11. Repeat the process until you have four 7-layer stacks of crêpes and cream. Dust powdered sugar on top of each stack and serve immediately.

Crêpes Suzette

4

This may be the most famous crêpe recipe in the world. Made with orange liqueur and orange juice, you'll find it in fine restaurants and cafes everywhere—and in your very own kitchen!

INGREDIENTS

3 tablespoons sugar

2 tablespoons butter

4 oranges, peeled and cut into slices

1 tablespoon orange liqueur

1 batch crêpes (page 108), cooked, stacked and covered in a clean kitchen cloth

PREPARATION

1. Heat a large saucepan over medium heat. Add the sugar, butter, and half of the orange slices, stirring to combine.

2. Increase the heat to high and cook until the sauce is light and the fruit pieces start breaking up.

3. Remove the saucepan from the heat and gently stir in the orange liqueur and remaining oranges.

4. To serve, place 1 crêpe on a serving dish and top with a spoonful of orange sauce.

5. Fold the crêpe in half, add another spoonful of sauce and fold again into quarters.

6. Repeat this process with the remaining crêpes and sauce. Serve immediately.

Choco Hazelnut Cream Crêpes

Serves

This chocolate sauce may be made well in advance and stored in the refrigerator for up to 1 week. Just before serving, it can be reheated in the microwave or in a bowl over a pan with boiling water.

INGREDIENTS

½ cup heavy cream

8 ounces unsweetened chocolate, cut into chunks

1 batch crêpes (page 108), cooked, stacked and covered in a clean kitchen cloth

½ cup chocolate hazelnut spread

PREPARATION

1. In a small saucepan over medium heat, bring the cream just to the boiling point.

2. Remove the cream from the heat and whisk in the chocolate until smooth. The cream can be used immediately, or refrigerated for up to 1 week.

3. To serve, place 1 crêpe on a serving dish. Spread thick lines of chocolate hazelnut spread and chocolate cream onto each crêpe.

4. Roll, fold, or wrap the crêpe as desired.

5. Repeat the process with the rest of the crêpes and serve.

Mixed Seafood Crêpes

For a light summer supper, serve this delicious dish with a side salad and a glass of sparkling water. If fresh seafood is hard to find, frozen seafood will do just fine.

INGREDIENTS

1 tablespoon olive oil

½ cooking onion, finely chopped

1 clove garlic, crushed

¼ cup white wine

⅓ cup heavy cream

1 teaspoon salt

½ teaspoon white pepper

2 pounds mixed seafood

1 batch crêpes (page 108), cooked, stacked and covered in a clean kitchen cloth

When making crêpes for savory dishes, remember to omit the sugar and vanilla.

PREPARATION

1. Heat a large, deep saucepan over medium heat. Add the olive oil, onion and garlic. Sauté, stirring occasionally, for 3 to 5 minutes until onion is soft.

2. Add the wine and cook, until the sauce is reduced by half.

3. Add the heavy cream, salt and pepper. Cook until sauce thickens slightly.

4. Mix in the seafood and cook, until seafood is cooked through and sauce thickens.

5. Remove from the heat and set aside.

6. To serve, place 1 crêpe on your work surface and spoon about 3 tablespoons of seafood mixture in the center of the crêpe. Roll into a cone shape.

7. When rolling the crêpe, hold the bottom ends close together so that the sauce is kept inside.

8. Repeat this process to fill and roll the rest of the crêpes and serve immediately.

Rich Ratatouille Crêpes

This wrapped Mediterranean entrée is lovely at lunch on a chilly winter day. The filling can be prepared a day in advance.

INGREDIENTS

⅛ cup + ⅛ cup olive oil

2 carrots, cut into ¼ inch dice

1 zucchini, cut into ¼ inch dice

1 eggplant, cut into ¼ inch dice

1 clove garlic, crushed

½ cup tomato juice

1 teaspoon salt

½ teaspoon ground black pepper

1 teaspoon finely chopped fresh thyme leaves

1 batch crêpes (page 108), cooked, stacked and covered in a clean kitchen cloth

Fresh oregano, for garnish

When making crêpes for savory dishes, remember to omit the sugar and vanilla.

PREPARATION

1. In a large frying pan over medium heat, heat ⅛ cup of oil. Add the carrots and sauté until golden.

2. Place a colander over a bowl. Using a slotted spoon, transfer the carrots from the pan to the colander.

3. Add the zucchini to the same pan and sauté until golden. Transfer to the colander with the slotted spoon.

4. Add the remaining ⅛ cup of oil, as well as the oil that drained off the sautéed vegetables, to the frying pan. Mix in the eggplant and sauté until golden.

5. With the slotted spoon, transfer the eggplant to the colander and let it sit for a few moments to drain.

6. Discard the oil remaining in the frying pan and wipe the pan with a paper towel. Transfer the vegetables from the colander to the pan, add the garlic and sauté for about 1 minute.

7. Mix in the tomato juice, salt, pepper and thyme until combined, then cook over low heat for 3 minutes, stirring occasionally.

8. To serve, place 1 crêpe on your work surface and spoon about 3 tablespoons of the mixture on the middle third of the crêpe.

9. Fold up the bottom of the crêpe to cover the filling and then fold over one side. Roll the crêpe towards the other side so that the entire filling is securely wrapped. Cut the crêpe in half.

10. Repeat to fill and roll the rest of the crêpes, garnish with oregano, and serve immediately.

Assorted Cheese Crêpes

4

Make sure the crêpes are warm when you serve this dish, so that the cheese softens and the flavor is released. Serve with a glass of fine wine.

INGREDIENTS

½ cup crumbled feta cheese

¼ cup grated parmesan cheese

¼ cup grated Gouda cheese

1 cup frozen corn kernels

1 tablespoon smoked Spanish paprika

1 batch crêpes (page 108), cooked, stacked and covered in a clean kitchen cloth

½ cup grated cheddar cheese

When making crêpes for savory dishes, remember to omit the sugar and vanilla.

PREPARATION

1. In a large bowl, mix together the feta, parmesan, Gouda, corn, and paprika until evenly combined.

2. Place a crêpe on your work surface and spoon 2 tablespoons of the cheese mixture on top.

3. Fold the crêpe in half and place on a serving dish.

4. Repeat this process with the remaining crêpes. Sprinkle with cheddar and serve.

Mushroom & Herb Crêpes

Serves

8

Great for entertaining, the filling in this dish can be made up to one day in advance and refrigerated until you are ready to serve it. When assembling the crêpes, make sure to leave some of the filling exposed.

INGREDIENTS

1 teaspoon olive oil

2 garlic cloves, crushed

1 pound fresh button mushrooms, halved

½ pound fresh Portobello mushrooms, halved

½ teaspoon salt

½ teaspoon ground white pepper

¼ cup white wine

2 tablespoons butter

1 batch crêpes (page 108), cooked, stacked and covered in a clean kitchen cloth

Fresh sage, for garnish

When making crêpes for savory dishes, remember to omit the sugar and vanilla.

PREPARATION

1. Heat a large saucepan over medium heat. Add the olive oil and garlic and sauté for about 2 minutes.

2. Mix in all the mushrooms and sauté for 3 minutes, stirring occasionally. Add the salt, pepper and wine, increase the heat to high and cook for 3 minutes.

3. Add the butter and cook for 2 minutes, then remove the saucepan from the heat and set aside.

4. To serve, place a crêpe on a serving dish and top with 2 tablespoons of the mushroom mixture.

5. Fold the crêpe in half, then top with another crêpe, 2 more tablespoons of the mushroom mixture and fold in half again.

6. Repeat this process to prepare all the crêpes. Drizzle extra sauce on top, garnish with sage and serve.

Ceviche Crêpes with Crème Fraîche

Each of the main elements in this recipe has a distinct flavor. When combined, they create a gourmet dish that is sure to draw accolades and requests for more!

INGREDIENTS

1½ pounds fresh fish fillets (halibut, sea bass, snapper), cut into ½-inch dice

⅓ cup fresh lime juice

3 tablespoons finely chopped shallots

2 red chili peppers, finely chopped

¼ cup coriander leaves, finely chopped

1 teaspoon salt

1 batch crêpes (page 108), cooked, stacked, and covered with a kitchen cloth

⅓ cup crème fraîche

2 tablespoons extra-virgin olive oil, for drizzling

When making crêpes for savory dishes, remember to omit the sugar and vanilla.

PREPARATION

1. In a large bowl, combine the fish, lime juice, shallots, chili peppers, coriander and salt.

2. Cover with plastic wrap and set aside for at least 15, and no more than 45 minutes.

3. To serve, place a crêpe on your work surface and spread with crème fraîche.

4. Scatter 1½ tablespoons of the fish mixture on top and then drizzle with olive oil.

5. Repeat this process with the rest of the crêpes and serve immediately.

Anchovy & Dried Tomato Crêpes

4

*Prepare an elegant Mediterranean brunch dish with this easy recipe.
Put on some Spanish music and you'll feel as though you've taken a trip
to the Iberian Peninsula.*

INGREDIENTS

2 tablespoons anchovies

1 tablespoon olive oil

1 cup oil-packed sun-dried tomatoes, drained and cut into thin strips

3 tablespoons finely chopped fresh parsley

1 batch crêpes (page 108), cooked, stacked, and covered with a kitchen cloth

---

When making crêpes for savory dishes, remember to omit the sugar and vanilla.

PREPARATION

1. Heat a large saucepan over low heat. Add the anchovies and olive oil and cook for about 3 minutes, until the anchovies melt into the oil.

2. Mix in the dried tomatoes until thoroughly combined and continue cooking for 3 minutes. Remove from the heat and mix in the parsley.

3. To serve, top each crêpe with a tablespoon of the anchovy mixture. Fold the crêpes loosely and serve immediately.

Savory Herb Crêpes

Serves

10

This striking dish is beautiful, aromatic and delicious! Wrap each crêpe around a filling of fresh baby salad leaves for a California-style appetizer.

INGREDIENTS

2 large eggs

2 tablespoons melted butter, plus more for greasing

1 cup cold milk

½ teaspoon salt

1 cup all-purpose white flour

¼ cup finely chopped fresh parsley

1 tablespoon finely chopped fresh chives

½ tablespoon fresh thyme leaves

¼ pound fresh baby salad leaves

When making crêpes for savory dishes, remember to omit the sugar and vanilla.

PREPARATION

1. In a large bowl, combine the eggs, melted butter, milk and salt. Sift in the flour and stir until batter is thick and smooth.

2. Cover with plastic wrap and refrigerate for 30 minutes.

3. Stir in the parsley, chives and thyme.

4. Heat a large crêpe pan over medium heat. Brush the pan with oil once it is warm.

5. Using a small ladle, pour about 3 tablespoons of batter into the pan. Use the back of the ladle to spread the batter in a circular motion, from the middle to the edges, so that the mixture covers the pan evenly.

6. Cook the crêpe for about 2 to 3 minutes, or until the edges draw away from the sides of the pan and the top is moist but not runny. Insert an offset spatula under the crêpe and check that the bottom is a light golden color.

7. Flip over the crêpe and cook on the other side for another 2 to 3 minutes, until light gold. Transfer the crêpe to a large plate and cover with a clean cloth.

8. Repeat with the remaining batter. Serve immediately or store, covered with a clean cloth, until ready to serve.

9. To serve, place each crêpe on a serving dish, lay a few baby salad leaves along the middle and then roll up. Repeat with the rest of the crêpes and serve.

Roasted Chicken & Corn Crêpes

Serves

4

In this dish, crêpes are used instead of traditional tortillas to wrap freshly grilled chicken breasts and corn. Spicy, attractive and delicious!

INGREDIENTS

1½ pounds chicken breast, cut into thin 2-inch strips

1½ cups frozen corn kernels

1 tablespoon ground smoked chipotle pepper

1 teaspoon salt

1 tablespoon olive oil

2 tablespoons coarsely chopped fresh marjoram or coriander

1 batch crêpes (page 108), cooked, stacked and covered in a clean kitchen cloth

When making crêpes for savory dishes, remember to omit the sugar and vanilla.

PREPARATION

1. Preheat the oven to 400°F.

2. In a deep pan, combine the chicken, corn, pepper, salt and olive oil. Bake for about 15 minutes or until chicken is cooked through.

3. Remove the pan from the oven and mix in the marjoram or coriander.

4. Place 1 crêpe on your work surface and top with a few pieces of chicken. Add 1 or 2 tablespoons of the corn mixture on top and then fold in half.

5. Repeat this process with the rest of the crêpes and serve immediately.

Chili Con Carne Crêpes

4

Crêpes can be surprisingly versatile—and this recipe is the perfect example. It's sure to inspire you to use homemade wrappers for other savory dishes.

INGREDIENTS

1 tablespoon olive oil

1 Bermuda onion, finely chopped

1 clove garlic, finely chopped

1½ pounds ground beef

1 teaspoon salt

½ teaspoon freshly ground black pepper

2 teaspoons smoked Spanish paprika

2 fresh tomatoes, finely grated

One 15-ounce can of red kidney beans in tomato juice

1 batch crêpes (page 108), cooked, stacked and covered in a clean kitchen cloth

---

When making crêpes for savory dishes, remember to omit the sugar and vanilla.

PREPARATION

1. In a large saucepan over medium heat, heat the olive oil, onion and garlic. Cook for 2 minutes or until the onions are soft.

2. Add the beef, salt, pepper and paprika. Cook for 5 minutes, stirring occasionally, until the beef is golden.

3. Add the tomatoes and beans, reduce the heat to low and cook for another 10 minutes.

4. To serve, place 1 crêpe on a serving dish and top with a few spoonfuls of the beef mixture. Fold the crêpes in half or leave open.

5. Repeat this process with the rest of the crêpes and serve immediately.

Metric Equivalents

The recipes that appear in this cookbook use the standard United States method for measuring liquid and dry or solid ingredients (teaspoons, tablespoons, and cups). The information on this chart is provided to help cooks outside the U.S. successfully use these recipes. All equivalents are approximate.

METRIC EQUIVALENTS FOR DIFFERENT TYPES OF INGREDIENTS

A standard cup measure of a dry or solid ingredient will vary in weight depending on the type of ingredient. A standard cup of liquid is the same volume for any type of liquid. Use the following chart when converting standard cup measures to grams (weight) or milliliters (volume).

Standard Cup	Fine Powder (ex. flour)	Grain (ex. rice)	Granular (ex. sugar)	Liquid Solids (ex. butter)	liquid (ex. milk)
1	140 g	150 g	190 g	200 g	240 ml
¾	105 g	113 g	143 g	150 g	180 ml
⅔	93 g	100 g	125 g	133 g	160 ml
½	70 g	75 g	95 g	100 g	120 ml
⅓	47 g	50 g	63 g	67 g	80 ml
¼	35 g	38 g	48 g	50 g	60 ml
⅛	18 g	19 g	24 g	25 g	30 ml

USEFUL EQUIVALENTS FOR DRY INGREDIENTS BY WEIGHT

(To convert ounces to grams, multiply the number of ounces by 30.)

1 oz	=	¹⁄₁₆ lb	=	30 g
4 oz	=	¼ lb	=	120 g
8 oz	=	½ lb	=	240 g
12 oz	=	¾ lb	=	360 g
16 oz	=	1 lb	=	480 g

USEFUL EQUIVALENTS FOR LENGTH

(To convert inches to centimeters, multiply the number of inches by 2.5.)

1 in				=	2.5 cm		
6 in	=	½ ft		=	15 cm		
12 in	=	1 ft		=	30 cm		
36 in	=	3 ft	=	1 yd	=	90 cm	
40 in				=	100 cm	=	1 m

USEFUL EQUIVALENTS FOR DRY INGREDIENTS BY WEIGHT

¼ tsp					=		1 ml	
½ tsp					=		2 ml	
1 tsp					=		5 ml	
3 tsp	=	1 tbls			½ fl oz =		15 ml	
		2 tbls	=	⅛ cup =	1 fl oz =		30 ml	
		4 tbls	=	¼ cup =	2 fl oz =		60 ml	
		5 ⅓ tbls	=	⅓ cup =	3 fl oz =		80 ml	
		8 tbls	=	½ cup =	4 fl oz =		120 ml	
		10 ⅔ tbls	=	⅔ cup =	5 fl oz =		160 ml	
		12 tbls	=	¾ cup =	6 fl oz =		180 ml	
		16 tbls	=	1 cup =	8 fl oz =		240 ml	
		1 pt	=	2 cups =	16 fl oz =		480 ml	
		1 qt	=	4 cups =	32 fl oz =		960 ml	
				=	33 fl oz =	1000 ml	= 1 liter	

USEFUL EQUIVALENTS FOR COOKING/OVEN TEMPERATURES

	Fahrenheit	Celsius	Gas Mark
Freeze Water	32° F	0° C	
Room Temperature	68° F	20° C	
Boil Water	212° F	100° C	
Bake	325° F	160° C	3
	350° F	180° C	4
	375° F	190° C	5
	400° F	200° C	6
	425° F	220° C	7
	450° F	230° C	8
Broil			Grill

Index